A BIRDKEEPER'S GUIDE TO

COCKATIELS

Practical advice on the care and accommodation of
these popular birds, plus a survey of colour forms

David Alderton

Publised

A Salamander Book

© 1989 Salamander Books Ltd.,
52 Bedford Row,
London WC1R 4LR,
United Kingdom.

ISBN 0 86101 444 8

Distributed in the UK by Hodder and Stoughton Services,
P.O.Box 6, Mill Road, Dunton Green, Sevenoaks, Kent TN13 2XX

Author

David Alderton has kept and bred a wide variety of birds for twenty five
years. He has travelled extensively in pursuit of this interest, visiting other
enthusiasts in various parts of the world, including the United
States, Canada and Australia. He has previously written a number of
books on avicultural subjects, and contributes regularly to general and
specialist publications in the UK and overseas. David studied veterinary
medicine at Cambridge University, and now, in addition to writing,
runs a highly respected international service that offers advice on the
needs of animals kept in both domestic and commercial environments.
He is also a Council Member of the Avicultural Society.

Photographer

Cyril Laubscher has been interested in aviculture and ornithology for more
than thirty years and has travelled extensively in Europe,
Australia and Southern Africa photographing wildlife. When he left
England for Australia in 1966 as an enthusiastic aviculturalist,
this fascination found expression as he began to portray birds
photographically. In Australia he met the well-known aviculturalist
Stan Sindel and, as a result of this association, seventeen of Cyril's
photographs were published in Joseph Forshaw's original book on
Australian Parrots in 1969. Since then, his photographs have met with
considerable acclaim and the majority of those that appear here
were taken specially for this book.

Credits

Editor: Vera Rogers Designer: Stuart Watkinson
Colour reproductions: Contemporary Lithoplates Ltd.
Filmset: Gee Graphics.
Printed in Belgium by Proost International Book Production

Contents

Above: *A tame cockatiel makes a delightful pet*
Overleaf: *White-faced pearl cock with primrose pied cock*

Introduction

The earliest reference to the cockatiel dates back to 1792, when it was described for scientific purposes. However, it was probably not until the late 1830s that cockatiels were first brought to Europe – at about the same time as the budgerigar – and for many years the cockatiel remained in the shadow of that other popular member of the Australian parrot family. Not until the 1950s did cockatiel mutations start to appear, and during recent years the cockatiel has finally achieved a strong international following, with numerous colours established and new colour combinations still being developed. As its popularity increased, cockatiel enthusiasts founded specialist societies that attract an international membership, and in the United States exhibition standards have been established for normal and colour forms. The cockatiel is classified as a member of the cockatoo family and was originally named the cockatoo parrot. The word cockatiel may have been introduced by a London bird

dealer who shortened the Dutch word 'Kakatielje', which translates as 'small cockatoo'.

The attraction of the cockatiel is not hard to understand. These birds are neither noisy nor destructive and will live and breed in colonies. With their gentle nature, they can be housed in a mixed collection alongside other birds, even tiny finches. As pets, cockatiels can be taught to talk and whistle, and become very attached to their owners. They have a longer lifespan than the budgerigar and are less expensive and easier to handle than a cockatoo. In this book we examine all aspects of housing cockatiels in the home or garden. Further chapters examine the feeding, health care and breeding of cockatiels. An introduction to the basic rules of genetics that govern the inheritance of specific colours and markings is followed by a survey of the increasing number of colour varieties currently available to the birdkeeper.

Choosing a cockatiel

There are various ways of obtaining a cockatiel. Your local pet shop may have some available, or you could contact a cage bird society near you to find a local breeder. Your library should be able to assist in finding the address of the club secretary, if you encounter difficulties. Various birdkeeping journals are available on subscription, or from newsagents, and these will almost certainly carry advertisements from breeders offering surplus stock. This may be especially useful if you are seeking one of the more unusual colours, which may be difficult to obtain locally.

If you wish to breed a particular colour, do not necessarily assume that it will cost you a great deal of money. With a knowledge of the genetics of the mutation concerned, you may be able to produce the colour without great expense. For example, the dominant silver mutation is at present one of the scarcest, and therefore costly to acquire, but to breed silvers you need only buy one bird of this colour, and could even pair it with a normal grey, at a considerable financial saving (see *Cockatiel genetics* page 61).

Colour mutations should be no harder to look after or breed than the normal grey form of the cockatiel. It is simply a matter of scarcity value. By looking in a birdkeeping journal, you will also be able to assess the relative costs of the different colours. Because cockatiels are normally prolific birds, the cost of acquiring new colours is likely to fall significantly over the course of several years, as more birds of a particular variety become available.

Choosing a young bird

If you are buying a cockatiel as a pet, you must obtain a young bird. It is usual to separate chicks from their parents when they are about seven weeks old. By this stage, the youngsters will be able to feed themselves and should settle quite readily into their new surroundings. Do not worry too much if the cockatiels appear rather nervous at this stage; the majority are still bred in aviary surroundings and are not accustomed to close human contact. They will settle down within a few weeks and develop into delightful pets.

Although hand-raising parrot chicks is more straightforward than it used to be, thanks to improved incubation equipment and the development of specially formulated rearing foods, it may still be difficult to find a young cockatiel reared by hand. This is simply a matter of economics; hand-raising is a very demanding occupation (see page 54), and the cost of the exercise, in terms of time, would vastly exceed the value of the cockatiel itself. If you are particularly keen to have a hand-raised chick, however, they are occasionally advertised in the birdkeeping magazines, usually because they have been neglected by their parents.

Alternatively, you can contact one of the hand-rearing services that also advertise, and enquire about availability. They will almost certainly be able to help you if you agree to place a firm order. Such businesses often rear the chicks of parrot breeders who lack the time to undertake this task themselves, and so will be well placed to obtain either eggs to hatch, or a very young cockatiel. Having been reared in close contact with people, such birds show no fear of humans.

If you are looking for aviary stock, you will have a wide choice of birds. In either case, the best time to obtain cockatiels is probably in the late summer, when there should be a good selection of youngsters on offer.

There are several advantages in purchasing young cockatiels as breeding stock. First, you will know the age of the birds, even if they are not banded. In adult cockatiels, only the presence around the leg of a closed ring – a continuous circular band, usually of aluminium – will confirm their age beyond doubt. Such rings can only be fitted over a period of a few days while the

or, especially in the case of lutinos, proved to be feather-pluckers, removing feathers from their chicks before these leave the nest.

If you buy recently fledged cockatiels, they should breed during the following year, so no time is lost by choosing young birds. They also tend to be slightly cheaper than adult pairs. Ideally, wait until the youngsters are about six months old and moulting for the first time. At this stage, you will be able to recognize pairs with certainty; at less than six months, it is harder to separate the sexes.

Sexing cockatiels

By observing a group of young cockatiels, it is often possible to identify cock birds quite early on. They tend to be more vocal, warbling away to themselves, and they may have brighter facial markings and larger crests. These latter indicators are not entirely reliable, however, but may help in some cases. Most people seeking a pet cockatiel prefer to have a young cock because, once adult, they may be more colourful (depending on the variety) and sing more readily than hens. Yet female cockatiels can become exceedingly devoted to their owners and are quite capable of talking.

The only reliable method of distinguishing the sex of a young cockatiel at fledging is by chromosomal karyotyping (see page 52). It is not commonly available or widely used, but can be of value in establishing certain mutations. Similarly, it is often possible to sex the chicks on the basis of coloration, when working with the sex-linked mutations.

Adult birds can usually be sexed visually; most hens retain the characteristic barring on the underside of the tail.

Choosing a healthy bird

Even if you are buying a young cockatiel as a pet, it always pays to look at all the birds carefully before making a choice. The coloration of youngsters can alter as they grow older, since all young birds tend to

Above: *A normal grey cockatiel with a lively, alert appearance. The ring on the foot will help to determine the age of the bird.*

cockatiels are still in the nest (see page 57). After this, the toes become too large to permit the passage of the ring over them. The information on a ring may include the breeder's initials, plus an individual number. The year of hatching is usually engraved across the band in an abbreviated form, such as '89', for example.

Although cockatiels may continue to breed successfully well into their teens, their fertility tends to decline with age. Furthermore, few breeders will part with their best breeding stock except, possibly, at a premium price. Older cockatiels offered for sale may, therefore, have been poor parents

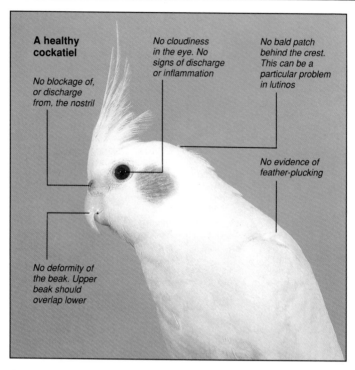

A healthy cockatiel

No blockage of, or discharge from, the nostril

No cloudiness in the eye. No signs of discharge or inflammation

No bald patch behind the crest. This can be a particular problem in lutinos

No evidence of feather-plucking

No deformity of the beak. Upper beak should overlap lower

Above: *A lutino cockatiel in fine condition. This colour form has become one of the most popular.*

resemble adult hens. Some features are consistent, however, such as the pattern of markings on pied cockatiels, which simply vary between individuals. When assessing lutinos, bear in mind that chicks with the darkest coloration in nest feather should moult into well-coloured adults, whose plumage is rich lemon, rather than a pale yellowish shade of white.

If you are interested in a specific cockatiel, ask the vendor to catch it for you, so you can examine it more closely. Start by looking at the head. The eyes should open readily, showing no signs of inflammation or discharge, nor should the eye itself appear to have a milky white glaze over its surface. Under these circumstances, the bird's vision is likely to be seriously impaired, if it is not actually blind. Red-eyed individuals may suffer from this complaint more than

those with dark eyes. Nor should the nostrils show any signs of discharge. If the cockatiel has been caught from an aviary, you may notice a minor abrasion on the cere, the fleshy area surrounding the nostrils. This seems to be the part of the body that cockatiels are most likely to injure if they fly directly into the aviary mesh, but small cuts generally heal rapidly and uneventfully.

Look at the feathering on the head, especially in lutino cockatiels. These birds may have a bald patch of variable size behind the crest. This is a genetic flaw and no feather growth will ever occur in this region. Evidence of feather plucking, however, is most often noticeable at the base of the neck and top of the wings, even extending further over the body; in these cases you should see new feathers sprouting through the skin. These appear as spikes at first, until their outer covering is lost and they unfurl into place. Again, this problem is most commonly associated with lutinos. Some strains of lutino are more predisposed to this vice than others, but there is no clear evidence of a genetic link. The plumage of affected youngsters grows again normally but, in terms of temperament, such birds may be more nervous in later life.

Nestlings, especially of the lighter-coloured varieties, may emerge with soiled, brownish tail feathers, a situation made worse in an aviary with an earth floor, as the birds will inevitably be attracted to it. This is no cause for concern, however, as the plumage may come clean when the cockatiels have the opportunity to bathe in a shower of rain. Alternatively, you can wash the cockatiel. This procedure will be essential if you plan to show the bird at this early age (see page 20), although the feathers will eventually be replaced when the bird moults.

Check the beak and claws as part of a routine inspection. If they are malformed in any way, they may need to be cut back regularly throughout the cockatiel's life. In the case of the beak, the top part should overlap the lower, but occasionally it may actually fit inside. In such a case, the cutting edges fail to meet, so that the lower part of the beak becomes abnormally long, even to the point of restricting the cockatiel's ability to feed properly. Where the beak is 'undershot' in this fashion, the only option is to trim the lower portion, perhaps every two months or so. There is no means of correcting such deformities. Some breeders feel that genetic factors may be involved, so that such cockatiels are best kept just as pets, rather than as breeding birds.

Similarly, instead of curving round normally, a claw can project at an abnormal angle, often in a vertical plane. An injury, or possibly an accumulation of nest dirt on the toe, may account for this problem and the claw will require regular trimming. An absence of claws is also significant if you are planning to show your birds at any stage,

because this deficiency will invariably be marked down by most judges. However, such cockatiels can prove very useful for breeding purposes, so it is not necessarily a major handicap.

Apart from the cockatiel's state of alertness, you can also assess its condition by running your finger along its breastbone. This is located in the midline of the lower chest and should feel like a slight bony prominence, with plump muscles on either side. If there is a distinct hollow here, and you can clearly feel the sides of the bone, this might suggest that the bird is not eating properly, especially if it has recently been separated from its parents. Check the food pot in its quarters to see if the seed is being properly dehusked.

Alternatively, especially in an older cockatiel, it is often a sign of illness, which may or may not be infectious. A heavy burden of intestinal parasitic worms, to which cockatiels are prone, could also account for weight loss. Always ask when a cockatiel was last dewormed before you buy it, and take precautions before introducing new stock to an established aviary, because of the ease with which these parasites can be spread via new arrivals (see page 46). Any signs of a digestive disturbance may be revealed by greenish staining of the plumage around the vent. This can often explain weight loss in older cockatiels.

Never be tempted to buy birds unless you are certain they are healthy. It may not always be possible to cure them and such cockatiels do represent a threat to the health of other birds in the collection. Cockatiels are more likely to fall ill when moved to new surroundings, because of the stress involved. Be prepared to keep them apart from other birds for a fortnight or so. During this time you can treat them for possible parasites and, once you are certain that they have settled down properly, you can release them into the flight. (See also Health care page 46-51.)

Whenever you acquire – or part with – a cockatiel, be sure to discuss its diet. This applies especially to recently fledged youngsters. They are more susceptible to digestive problems following a change in diet than adult birds. If, for example, they have been receiving a special rearing food, be sure that you have a supply available, at least for the first few days, while your new acquisition settles in with you.

Buying one or more cockatiels is not something to be undertaken lightly. With luck, you will be acquiring a bird that will be part of your daily life for, perhaps, twenty years or so. Therefore, if you are at all uncertain about a particular individual, do not feel pressured into accepting it. Because cockatiels are now so widely bred, you should find no shortage of suitable birds on offer.

Catching and handling

The easiest way to catch a cockatiel in a cage is to place one hand on the back of the bird, using the thumb and little finger to restrain the wings. Then gently hold the cockatiel's head between the first and second fingers, but never apply direct pressure, because obviously you could squeeze the bird's windpipe, with potentially fatal consequences.

Once adequately restrained in this way, the cockatiel usually stops struggling, but it may nip one of your fingers quite painfully, so it is sensible to wear a thin pair of gloves for protection, at least until you are used to handling cockatiels on a regular basis.

Catching cockatiels in an aviary is more difficult, because the birds are quite fast and certainly agile in flight. Some breeders prefer to use a net to catch individual birds, but it must be well padded around the rim; otherwise, if you catch the cockatiel clumsily, you could stun, or even kill it. Proper catching nets are available from pet shops, or from the specialist suppliers who frequently advertise in the birdkeeping magazines.

Before attempting to catch a cockatiel in the aviary, it is a good idea to take down the perches, so that they cannot obstruct your movement. The birds then fly onto the aviary mesh, holding on with their claws. It is easier to net them in this position, rather than to try and catch them in flight. Catching nets are usually quite broad and deep, so that once the bird is inside, you can restrain it by holding the material just below the rim for a few seconds. Then, by resting the net face down on the aviary floor, you will have both hands free to transfer the cockatiel either to a cage or box. Restrain the bird in one hand, as described on this page, and once you have virtually removed it from the net, use your free hand to prise its claws out of the material of the net. Once caught, a cockatiel always clenches its feet onto any available surface to obtain a grip. If you are unaware of this, you are likely to damage its claws, which could begin to bleed as a result.

Below: *A cockatiel can give a painful peck if handled carelessly. It is often best to wear thin cotton gloves until you are confident about restraining these birds properly.*

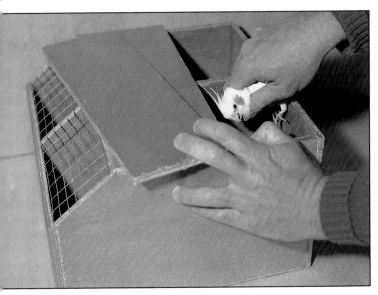

Above: *It is safer to use a secure wooden box for transferring birds between flights or for bringing new stock home. Keep it clean and dry.*

Bringing your cockatiel home

A wooden travelling box is a useful piece of equipment that will be of value right from the outset. You may be able to buy a box from a specialist supplier, but you can easily build one yourself. Construct a simple plywood box, about 30cm(12in) square and 23cm(9in) high, held together with panel pins, but leave the front and back open at this stage. Cover the front with 2.5x1.25cm(1x0.5in) mesh, bent and tacked over the outer sides. A hinged door forms the other face and provides access. Close it with a latch on the top and add a small padlock for extra security.

The shallow height of this box should prevent the cockatiel from attempting to fly upwards once it is confined inside. Empty cardboard boxes are sometimes used for moving cockatiels, either from one aviary to another, or on a longer trip, but they have several disadvantages and are certainly not escape-proof. In containers such as these, birds may generate considerable force flying upwards into the folded flaps, where light may be visible. If the cockatiel can gain a foothold there, it will probably escape. The bottom of the box may also be a weak area; unless it is secure, the box may collapse under the bird's weight. If the ventilation holes are too large, the cockatiel, seeing a light, may start gnawing at the cardboard, which is unlikely to prove very resistant to its beak. With a proper wooden carrier, however, you can fix a handle on the top, and line the interior with folded sheets of newspaper, so that the base remains reasonably clean after it has been in use.

Never leave cockatiels alone in a car during hot weather, because the temperature inside can build up to a fatal level for the birds within minutes. Nor should you transport cockatiels in the car boot, in case exhaust fumes leak in here. Birds are extremely sensitive to carbon monoxide fumes and will rapidly die if exposed to them.

Except on a very long journey, there is no need to worry about providing water or food. However, if you think you might be delayed, you can fix a drinker to the wire mesh front and sprinkle some seed on the floor of the travelling box.

Cockatiels in the home

A wide array of cages is available today, but some are too elaborate and ornate for cockatiels. Circular designs, for example, often look very attractive, but actually allow the bird very little flying space. Choose the largest possible cage, because cockatiels are often more active than other parrots, preferring to fly, rather than climb around their quarters. Even if you let your pet fly around the room, it will remain fitter if housed in a large cage.

Rectangular cages are a better choice and you should be able to find a modular system without too much difficulty, now that increasing numbers of pet shops are stocking them. The flexibility of this system has great advantages; no longer do you have to buy a cage of a specific size; instead, you can obtain component parts that clip together so that you can design the enclosure yourself.

If you assemble your own cage, try to find space for a sectional rectangular unit 1.8m long and 0.9m high and wide (6x3x3ft). The mesh covering the panels should measure 2.5x1.25cm(1x0.5in) or 2.5cm(1in) square. Site the cage door centrally for easy access. With most units of this type it is possible to obtain a base tray incorporating a sliding component that can be pulled out, enabling you to clean the cockatiel's quarters easily.

An indoor cockatiel cage

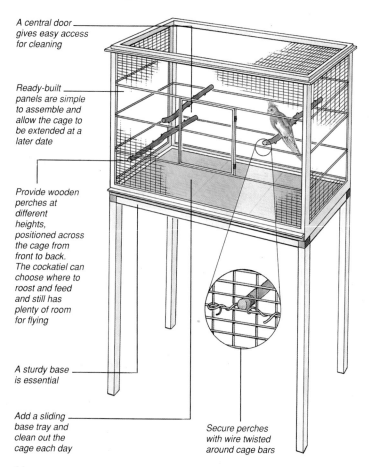

A central door gives easy access for cleaning

Ready-built panels are simple to assemble and allow the cage to be extended at a later date

Provide wooden perches at different heights, positioned across the cage from front to back. The cockatiel can choose where to roost and feed and still has plenty of room for flying

A sturdy base is essential

Add a sliding base tray and clean out the cage each day

Secure perches with wire twisted around cage bars

Simply replace the lining material, such as sheets of newspaper, thus removing the bird's droppings and seed husks without having to wash the tray every time. Regular, daily cleaning of the cage is always recommended, especially if you are feeding perishable foods.

Perches

Although some cages are equipped with perches, these are not always entirely suitable. Plastic perches are easy to clean if you scrub them in a bucket of water, but they are uncomfortable for cockatiels to grip and you may find that your bird spends most of its time perching on a seed pot or gripping the sides of its cage. Wooden perches cut from dowel rods are unusual these days, but they are more satisfactory. Even so, the cockatiel has no opportunity to nibble at the wood because it is very hard. Ideally, therefore, remove any plastic perches and always add fresh-cut branches to the cockatiel's quarters to help keep its beak in trim. As the bird gnaws them away, discard the shorter lengths and replace them.

Branches can be cut from various trees; sycamore is suitable and so is elder, with its relatively soft texture. Prunings from an apple tree are also useful as perches, but avoid collecting from areas that may have been sprayed with chemicals in case dangerous

Above: Arrange the perches so that the cockatiels can feed easily, thus minimizing wastage of seed. It is also helpful if the perches can be removed for washing, as they may become soiled by droppings.

residues remain in the wood.

Always wash all branches before placing them in the cage as they may have been soiled by wild birds, whose droppings could prove harmful to the cockatiel. Similarly, avoid dead wood that is likely to be contaminated with fungal spores.

A variation in the diameter of its perches will obviously encourage the cockatiel to exercise its toes. It will also help to ensure that pressure points do not develop on the underside of the feet, which may then become infected. The perch should be thick enough so that the claws of the front and rear toes do not curl round and touch each other, yet not so broad that the cockatiel has difficulty in gripping. There is no need to trim off smaller side branches, however, since your cockatiel will enjoy nibbling these.

In a flight cage, you should be able to include at least two perches quite comfortably. Position one at each end across the cage, from front to back, but leave enough space for the cockatiel to perch and turn round without rubbing its tail on the mesh. Obviously, it must

15

also have sufficient headroom to sit without crouching, so fix the upper perch at least 30cm(12in) from the top of the cage.

Although both perches can be positioned at the same height, it is better to place one lower than the other to encourage the cockatiel to fly up and down. It will usually prefer to roost on the upper perch, so place the food pots level with the lower one.

Depending partly on the size of the mesh covering the flight panels, you may be able to fit the perches in place simply by cutting a vertical or horizontal notch in each end. Provided you have measured the length accurately, it should be possible to hold the perch by the pressure of these notches fitting into the strands of mesh.

Alternatively, you can force the perches into position against the wire, but this distorts the shape of the cage and looks unsightly. The other option is to wire the ends in place. Twist a single strand of wire around each end of the perch, ensuring that it is tightly coiled so that there is no risk of the cockatiel becoming trapped by its foot. Then twist the loose ends around the mesh of the cage, being sure to leave the knot itself outside the bars. Here, the sharp cut edges will be out of the cockatiel's reach and cannot hurt the bird. This method ensures that the perches should remain firmly in place, with the weight being distributed over several strands of cage mesh.

Positioning the cage

The best position for the cockatiel cage is in a corner of a room close to a window, but never in direct sunlight. Here the bird will feel secure, knowing that it can only be approached from the front or from one side. Make sure that the cage is sufficiently high off the floor, at about eye-level if possible. This will make it easier for you to have contact with your pet and service its living quarters.

Even traditional square parrot cages are quite heavy and need a secure base. It may be possible to

Above: A typical cage for a cockatiel. The plastic base unit is attached to the wire-mesh top by clips at either end. To clean the cage thoroughly, separate the two components. Note the pink iodine nibble at the front of the cage.

obtain a stand, but these are not always very robust. In addition, if you have young children, it is safer to place the cage out of their reach on a solid piece of furniture, rather than risk them pulling the stand over. Larger cages may incorporate a built-in trolley underneath. This adds stability and ensures that the unit can be moved easily, because it is mounted on castors.

Potential hazards

During the warmer months of the year, you may decide to move the cockatiel into a conservatory, but do make sure that your pet is never exposed to temperatures over 32°C(90°F), otherwise the symptoms of heatstroke will soon become apparent. The cockatiel will sit with its wings held away from its body and its beak open, panting and thus trying to keep cool. If the bird is positioned in direct sunlight the consequences can be fatal.

Do not forget the other dangers that lurk here, as within any other room. The large expanse of glass in many conservatories is an obvious hazard because cockatiels do not instantly appreciate its presence. As a result, a bird may try to fly through this invisible barrier, stunning itself, or even breaking its neck as a result. In a room setting, it is sensible to cover the windows with net curtains before letting the cockatiel out of its cage, while in a conservatory you should create some sort of barrier if the cockatiel is flying free, or accidentally escapes from its cage.

In addition, all open windows should have a wire mesh screen over them to prevent the cockatiel from escaping and also to stop neighbourhood cats climbing through the opening and possibly harming your pet.

Cockatiels are usually keen to consume greenfood and in a conservatory – or even in a room in the house – you will probably have a variety of plants. Apart from the damage that may be caused to the plant if the cockatiel eats its leaves, there is always a risk that the bird could be poisoned. A number of houseplants are dangerous to

Dangers in the conservatory

Flaky paintwork may contain traces of lead that can poison cockatiels and other parrots

In direct sunlight at temperatures over 32°C(90°F) birds can rapidly succumb to effects of heatstroke

Birds are not always aware of clear glass; they may incur serious injury if they fly against a window

Protect open windows with a mesh covering to prevent accidental escapes and deter curious cats

A cage on castors is easy to move around; it may be necessary to lock the castors in place for safety

Remember that the cockatiel may be tempted to sample the leaves of a 'safe' but prized houseplant

Even if cats do not harm a pet bird directly, they can upset and frighten it quite severely

Before allowing cockatiels to fly freely, remove any plants with poisonous leaves or berries

cockatiels, including ivies (*Hedera* sp.) and the egg-plant (*Solanum*) with its orange-red berries. If the birds are allowed to fly around freely, keep them away from all such plants.

Old flaky paintwork can be equally dangerous if ingested, because it may contain traces of lead that accumulate in the body. Lead poisoning, either from paintwork or water, or indeed a combination of both, is not uncommon in parrotlike birds. It can result in weakness and loss of co-ordination. Unless you are

aware of this hidden danger, your cockatiel could succumb without you even being aware of the risk. Should your pipework include lead, it is safest to give your cockatiel filtered or bottled drinking water.

Other pets
Dogs generally ignore birds that share their home, but if they try to chase them then, clearly, they should be kept apart. Cats, on the other hand, are more likely to harm a pet bird, lurking in wait until the bird is out of its cage. Some are even bold enough to leap on top of the cockatiel's cage and attempt to reach it through the mesh. This may not cause direct harm, but it will certainly upset your bird, which may injure itself in the cage.

Below: *A young cockatiel should develop into a tame companion and will live for many years, but it may be a little nervous at first.*

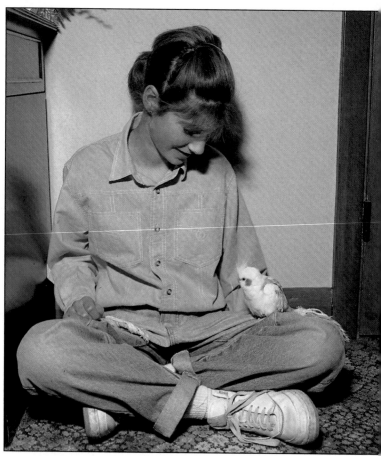

A tame bird is especially vulnerable to a cat, since its natural fear is lessened. If at all possible, therefore, keep your cockatiel in a room away from cats, and always check their whereabouts before letting the bird out of its cage. Never be tempted to leave the cockatiel unsupervised in the room, even for a short time, if you have children. They could open the door of the room and let the cat in while you are outside, and this could well spell the end for your bird.

Open fish tanks represent another hazard for a young cockatiel. If the bird falls into the water and its plumage becomes saturated, it will drown. Avoid this risk by placing a tray over the aquarium, even if you do not have a proper cover available.

If you already own a pet parrot belonging to another species you will need to introduce the new cockatiel very carefully, otherwise jealousy is inevitable. This can take various forms. The established bird may call loudly and persistently while you attend to the newcomer. If the cockatiel lands on top of its cage, the parrot is likely to bite its feet through the mesh. It will also attempt to do this if the cages are placed close together, side by side.

In order to reduce the risk of conflict, spend longer periods of time with your original pet. By letting both birds out together, signs of aggression are less likely to develop and in time the two members of the parrot family may develop a close bond, even roosting alongside each other in a cage. There is no risk of them producing chicks; even if eggs are laid, these will be infertile. Cockatiels have never been crossed successfully with any other parrot, because they have no close relations in the group.

The first few days
If possible, set up the cage before you collect your new pet. Place food containers near a perch and on the floor, so they are quite conspicuous and give the bird an opportunity to choose where it

Above: *It may be possible to buy a cover for the cockatiel's cage or you may have to make one. Accustom the bird to a period of darkness, lasting from the early evening until the following morning.*

feeds. In new surroundings and on its own for the first time, a young cockatiel may be reluctant to feed from a hopper (see page 45), but will eat seed provided in an open container at perch level.

After being released from the travelling box, the cockatiel may fly around rather wildly for a few seconds, before perching. Although it can be difficult if you have children, try to leave the bird alone in the room for an hour or so to settle down after the journey. Turn on the light before it gets dark. A young cockatiel accustomed to an outside aviary will not be used to sudden flashes of light and may panic, especially in an unfamiliar cage. This fear will pass in time, but during these early stages, avoid switching the light on and off repeatedly throughout the evening.

At first, the cockatiel's droppings are likely to be greenish, but once it starts to eat, these will firm up and darken in colour. You can check the amount of food being eaten by the presence of seed husks on the floor of the cage, since cockatiels only eat the kernels of seeds, not the outer casing.

On the second or third day, you can offer a little greenfood through the mesh of the cage. Hold it still and keep a slight distance away so that you do not overwhelm the

Above: *To tame a cockatiel, first persuade your pet to use your fingers as an alternative perch, by holding them outstretched.*

Above: *Moving slowly, gently touch the cockatiel's feet with your fingers, to encourage it to lift its feet and perch on your hand instead.*

cockatiel. It may refuse the food, and if it shows no interest within a few minutes, simply drop the greenstuff through the bars, on top of the seed. Sooner or later, the young bird should be attracted to eat it and in time will become eager to feed from your hand.

Taming your bird
The length of time it takes to tame your cockatiel depends firstly on how steady it was when you first acquired it. Hand-raised chicks will already be finger-tame and then it is a question of building on this existing bond. With aviary-bred cockatiels, the process will be more protracted. It also depends on how long you can spend with your cockatiel each day.

Allow a newly acquired youngster to settle in quietly for a week or so. During this time, you can offer a selection of greenstuff and fruit by hand, as suggested on page 19. Once the cockatiel is reasonably settled, you can open the cage door and offer food directly, holding it up for the cockatiel so it is within easy reach. Always move your hand slowly; fast, jerky movements will upset the bird. You may soon be able to induce it to perch on your hand.

Place the first two fingers of one hand parallel with the perch, close to the cockatiel's feet. Introduce your fingers from beneath the bird

and the level of the perch, as this approach will be less likely to scare it. Once your fingers are actually touching the toes, carefully and slowly run them up to the top of the foot. During this time, the cockatiel is likely to try to step off the perch onto your fingers.

Then, very carefully, you may be able to lift the bird a short distance off the perch while it remains on your hand. This is the critical stage and once it is reached, you will be well on the way to taming your cockatiel. You will need patience to repeat this process several times until the bird perches fearlessly on your hand. You will then be able to feed your pet at the same time, using your other hand. In time, the cockatiel will also allow you to tickle the back of its neck, which is a gesture of great trust.

Spraying your bird
From the outset, you should accustom your pet to being sprayed, although it may be nervous of the procedure at first. You will need a small plant sprayer with a fine nozzle that creates a mist of water droplets. Fill this with tepid water, and then remove the bird's seed pot from the cage, so the contents do not become damp. It may be worthwhile moving the cage to another room, so that surrounding furniture, for example, remains dry.

Above: *Once the bird is sitting on your fingers, you will already have a tame pet, but carry on with the same regular lessons.*

Above: *Do not forget to reward your pet. A tame cockatiel will perch readily on your hand and take food from your fingers.*

Wait until the cockatiel is perched quietly, and then press the handle of the sprayer several times in succession, keeping the nozzle itself pointed above the bird's head. The droplets will fall onto the cockatiel from above and the effect will be rather like a shower instead of a hose. Once it becomes used to it, your bird may actively solicit a spray by holding its wings outstretched and calling quite loudly, as do cockatiels bathing in a shower of rain outside. Apart from washing their plumage, the water also helps to dampen down feather dust, which may otherwise be

wafted into the air and can cause discomfort, particularly to asthma sufferers. Cockatiels produce more feather dust during the moult, so additional regular bathing could be useful at this stage. Surplus feather dust often collects on the floor around a cage, and can be wiped up using a damp cloth.

There is no need to soak your cockatiel when giving it a spray; a light covering of water droplets is

Below: *A regular spray with tepid water damps down feather dust, especially during the moult, and encourages your bird to preen.*

Wing clipping

Do not cut the
two outermost
primary feathers

Leave intact
some secondary
feathers close
to body

Primary
feathers

Secondary
feathers

sufficient. Saturating the plumage is likely to give the bird a chill, especially during the moulting period. Nor is there any need to dry the cockatiel after spraying.

If you have sprayed the bird in another room, move it back to its usual spot without delay. Never be tempted to keep a pet cockatiel in the kitchen for any length of time because fumes can prove fatal. This applies especially to those given off by non-stick cooking pans that overheat. In one instance, five cockatiels housed in a kitchen were all dead within half an hour, poisoned by such fumes.

Clipping your cockatiel's wing
This may sound a rather drastic step, but it can actually save your pet from injury while it becomes used to its new surroundings. Wing-clipping does not prevent the cockatiel from flying and is quite painless if carried out properly. It simply takes some of the power away, so that a collision with a window, for example, is less likely to have fatal consequences.

Once the cockatiel is tame, you may decide that wing-clipping is no longer necessary. It is then simply a matter of waiting until the next moult, when the clipped feathers will be shed and replaced by a new

Above: A fully flighted cockatiel is a magnificent sight, but wing clipping may be necessary, especially with a young bird in new surroundings. Take care that this procedure does not result in bleeding.

set, thus restoring the bird's full flying ability. Cockatiels, unlike many other pet parrots, are relatively fast fliers and more likely to injure themselves in a collision.

If you do decide to clip the flight feathers, you will need a pair of sharp scissors and an assistant to hold the bird for you. The thrust in flight comes from the long flight feathers, which are clearly visible when the wing is held open. Cut carefully in a straight line across the flight feathers, at the base of the feather vane, just before this narrows to join the shaft. In this way, there is no risk of bleeding; if you cut down across the shaft, you could cause haemorrhaging. The outermost two flight feathers are often left intact, so that the appearance of the wing is not affected when the wing is closed.

Power of mimicry
The cockatiel does not appear to be as talented a mimic as the budgerigar, but it can be taught quite a variety of phrases and

tends to have clearer diction. Cockatiels are certainly more versatile in that they soon learn to whistle tunes, probably because of their normal inclination to whistle individual notes. Repetition will play a vital part in teaching a cockatiel to talk or whistle, and you may want to use a cassette recorder to assist in the early stages.

You will probably want to choose a name for you cockatiel that it can learn to repeat. Names ending with a 'y', such as 'Freddy', seem to be the easiest for a bird to mimic. Try to establish a routine, for example by saying 'Good morning, Freddy' each day when you first enter the room. In the evening, it is a good idea to cover the cage with a suitable cloth, so that the cockatiel is not exposed to long periods of artificial light, which can interfere with the moulting process. You can therefore repeat 'Goodnight, Freddy' when you place the cover over the cage. Soon the cockatiel will come to associate these phrases with the specific events, and respond accordingly. Linking in with the training procedure, you can add 'Good boy, Freddy', every time the bird sits on your finger.

In this way, your bird will acquire a sensible vocabulary, rather than confused, inane chatter. If you want to teach longer sentences, break them down into short sections, adding a new phrase once the previous one has been learnt. You can even teach a cockatiel to repeat a whole nursery rhyme by this method.

Young birds are the most receptive, but once cockatiels have learnt to talk, they can continue to do so throughout their lives. Even cockatiels kept in outside aviaries may talk, and can learn to whistle simple tunes, especially if they were acquired as youngsters.

Toys
A number of toys marketed primarily for budgerigars are also suitable for pet cockatiels, but do ensure that they are sufficiently robust. Some plastic toys have sharp projections inside that can cause injury if exposed when the toy is broken. Generally, simple toys are best. Cockatiels often appreciate a mirror and ladders are also popular. Cockatiels do not like swings as much as budgerigars do, however, and if there is space, it is better to include an extra perch, rather than a swing.

A ping-pong ball can provide a cockatiel with useful stimulation, as the bird rolls it back and forth with its beak. When dirty, simply wipe the ball over with a damp piece of kitchen towelling. Many of the more elaborate toys are difficult to clean.

If you are out for long periods each day, leave a radio turned on as a source of companionship for the cockatiel. But beware – your pet may soon be repeating various jingles as a result!

Another option is to obtain a second cockatiel as a companion. Being naturally sociable birds, they live together quite happily in pairs, even if they are the same sex. Furthermore, there is rarely any difficulty in bringing cockatiels together, whereas cockatoos and other larger parrots may disagree violently when introduced.

Below: *Cockatiels are not usually aggressive birds, and you can keep two together without any serious risk of fighting. There are many colours to choose from – a pair of dominant silvers are shown here.*

Cockatiels in the garden

Cockatiels make very attractive aviary occupants and their musical calls are unlikely to upset close neighbours. Nevertheless, it is worth mentioning that you intend building an aviary, just in case there could be any objections. For a relatively small structure, there is probably no need to obtain official planning permission, especially if you are building it at the back of your property, away from the road. This is desirable in any event, since an aviary can present a target both for vandals and for thieves.

Planning restrictions do, however, limit the size of aviary that you can build, so if in doubt, check the regulations at your local planning office. Take a sketch of the site, showing the proposed position of the aviary and its approximate measurements, as well as those of the garden itself. If you do need to submit a formal application of any kind there will be a slight delay before you can proceed, but it is much better to take this step, rather than rush into building the aviary and then find you have to dismantle it.

First considerations
When deciding on the site, start by choosing a sheltered spot, out of the direction of prevailing winds. It should be reasonably sunny, and not overhung by trees, otherwise leaves are likely to fall onto the roof and broken branches could

Siting the aviary

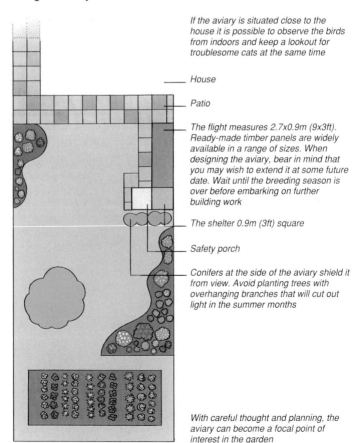

If the aviary is situated close to the house it is possible to observe the birds from indoors and keep a lookout for troublesome cats at the same time

_____ *House*

Patio

The flight measures 2.7x0.9m (9x3ft). Ready-made timber panels are widely available in a range of sizes. When designing the aviary, bear in mind that you may wish to extend it at some future date. Wait until the breeding season is over before embarking on further building work

The shelter 0.9m (3ft) square

Safety porch

Conifers at the side of the aviary shield it from view. Avoid planting trees with overhanging branches that will cut out light in the summer months

With careful thought and planning, the aviary can become a focal point of interest in the garden

Above: *A cockatiel aviary can become a striking feature of a landscaped garden. Do not include plants inside the flight, however.*

damage the structure itself. Furthermore, during the summer, the aviary is likely to be in relative darkness once the leaf buds have opened, and the droppings of wild birds perched in the trees are likely to contaminate the aviary from above and may introduce disease.

A pleasant position for the aviary is at the edge of an area of lawn. Here you will be able to sit outside and enjoy watching the birds on a warm summer's day. It also helps to choose a site that is clearly visible from indoors, so you can see the cockatiels from this angle as well. This can be especially important during the summer if you are troubled by neighbourhood cats and have to drive them off before they disturb the birds. Although you can deter cats by the design of the aviary (see page 37), some are extremely persistent and will only respond to direct intervention on your part.

There is probably no need to provide artificial lighting or heating for cockatiels, but under certain circumstances it may be desirable, especially if you work long hours during the winter and only see your birds after dark for much of the week. If you locate the aviary close to the house it will be cheaper to run an electrical supply to it.

It is quite possible, and certainly desirable, to integrate the aviary into the garden, so that it becomes an attractive feature. For this reason you may choose a site already occupied by a flower border, or a lawn area adjoining a fence. The drawback of this approach to planning is that it can restrict your ability to extend an existing aviary at a later date. Birdkeeping often proves to be an infectious hobby, and you should bear this in mind from the outset!

When deciding on the dimensions of the aviary, consider whether you want to keep just a single pair of cockatiels, or a group of these birds. The temptation will be to build a slightly larger structure and opt for breeding on the colony system. Although cockatiels can be housed quite satisfactorily in this way, breeding results are often not as good as when individual pairs are breeding on their own. Pairs may decide to share a nestbox, for

Above: *Cockatiels will live happily in a colony, but if you wish to breed birds of a particular colour, keep individual pairs together.*

example, so that eggs become chilled. Another point to remember is that you will have no control over the way the birds choose to mate, which is very important if you are hoping to breed chicks of a particular colour or colour combination. Nevertheless, if your prime object is to have an attractive group of birds in an aviary, rather than to breed from them, then a slightly larger structure is desirable.

The size of the aviary

Because most aviary mesh is approximately 90cm(36in) wide, aviaries are usually constructed on the basis of 90cm(36in) modular units. You can sometimes find mesh 120cm(48in) wide, and this will save on timber costs if you are planning a flight 3.6m(12ft) long. Instead of four 90cm(36in) panels, you will only need three panels, each measuring 120cm(48in) wide.

Although 180cm(6ft) mesh is available, this is less satisfactory because it tends to sag on the frame without a central support.

Being active birds, cockatiels will show to best effect in a flight measuring 3.6m(12ft) in length, although 2.7m(9ft) flights are adequate if space is limited. A height of 1.8m(6ft) should give you reasonably easy access, although you may want to increase this slightly if you are tall. This is not difficult and means, of course, that it should be easier for you to service the flight – and catch the cockatiels when necessary – without the risk of scalping yourself!

The width of the aviary is less critical, but if you are planning to keep more than one pair of cockatiels together, a useful guide would be to allow a minimum width of 90cm(36in) for each pair. In an aviary housing three breeding pairs, therefore, the flight needs to be 270cm(9ft) square. Higher stocking densities are possible, but the likelihood of breeding disappointments will increase.

Preparing the site

A secure base for the aviary is essential, not just to protect the structure in gales, but also to ensure that it does not start to rot prematurely. Start by removing any grass from the site, cutting away a wider area of turf than necessary because this is likely to be badly damaged during the building work. If you carefully cut the grass using a sharp spade and fold the turf inwards so that the roots are uppermost, you should be able to replant it satisfactorily later on. Keep it in a shaded spot and do not allow it to dry out at any stage.

Mark out the site carefully and dig trenches around the perimeter, to a depth of 45cm(18in). Set a course of blocks here, extending to a height of 30cm(12in) above ground. This provides the base on which the framework will ultimately be positioned.

The floor of the aviary

Before you reach this stage however, you will need to decide upon the floor covering. A concrete base in the shelter is the easiest to keep clean. Because cockatiels often forage for spilt seeds on the ground, it is important that the base of the flight can also be kept clean. A grass floor is therefore unsatisfactory; it will be very difficult to disinfect and if by any chance the cockatiels suffer with intestinal roundworms, you will find it impossible in such surroundings to prevent reinfection after treatment (see page 46).

If you opt for a concrete floor, start by digging down and removing the earth over the whole base, to a depth of 23cm(9in). Fill this with hardcore, such as old bricks, well compacted to a depth of 15cm(6in). Add a concrete and ballast mix on top and finally put a smooth slope on the floor so that rainwater will run off easily, rather than forming stale puddles over the surface.

Try to avoid adding too much sand to this final covering, otherwise in time the surface will become heavily colonized by algae, creating an unattractive green, slimy appearance. It will also

Preparing the site

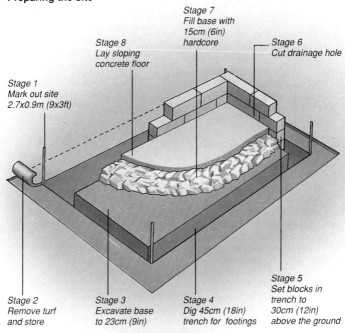

Stage 7
Fill base with
15cm (6in)
hardcore

Stage 8
Lay sloping
concrete floor

Stage 6
Cut drainage hole

Stage 1
Mark out site
2.7x0.9m (9x3ft)

Stage 2
Remove turf
and store

Stage 3
Excavate base
to 23cm (9in)

Stage 4
Dig 45cm (18in)
trench for footings

Stage 5
Set blocks in
trench to
30cm (12in)
above the ground

crumble quite easily after winter frosts. Unless you are a competent plasterer, it is probably best to ask a specialist to carry out this part of the job, leaving you an attractive, durable finish on the floor.

Paving slabs are a less permanent alternative to concrete and just as easy to wash down when necessary. Nevertheless, they should be mounted on a proper base, and carefully sloped for drainage purposes. Whether you lay a concrete base or paving stones, cut a small drainage hole in the blockwork surround at the lower point, so that water can be easily channelled from the aviary.

Some breeders still prefer to use coarse gravel as a floor lining in outside flights. However, it is important to lay a thick base – at least 12.5cm(5in) deep – otherwise the gravel may become saturated with rainwater in a heavy storm. You can place concrete slabs in the gravel beneath the perches where most of the droppings collect and scrape away the dirt with a spade. Some dirt will wash into the gravel base, however, but hopefully it will be out of reach of the cockatiels.

There is less risk of a parasitic infection in these surroundings than on a grass floor, but worm eggs can remain viable for a long time, especially hidden in a dark, damp environment, such as a bed of gravel. When you rake over the floor there is always the strong possibility that a number of eggs will be returned to the surface to reinfect the birds. A further major drawback of a gravel floor will become apparent when the cockatiels are moulting; it is very difficult to remove the feathers that will inevitably accumulate here.

Sectional structures
Building an aviary has been greatly simplified in recent years by the advent of flexible component systems. These enable you to construct an aviary to your own design, using a fully integrated set of doors, roof and side panels. Separate units are usually available to make up both the outer, wire

mesh part of the aviary, known as the flight, and the attached shelter.

Manufacturers of such systems advertise in the birdkeeping journals and, at first glance, there

Aviary for one pair of cockatiels

5cm (2in) – square timber frames are joined with bolts and washers

Site the aviary in a sheltered spot

A sloping concrete floor is easy to keep clean

may seem to be quite a wide variation in price. On closer examination you will find that some firms charge extra for weather-proofing the woodwork and for delivery, while others may offer a jointed framework, which proves more stable than a unit in which the lengths of wood are simply nailed together. Check on these various

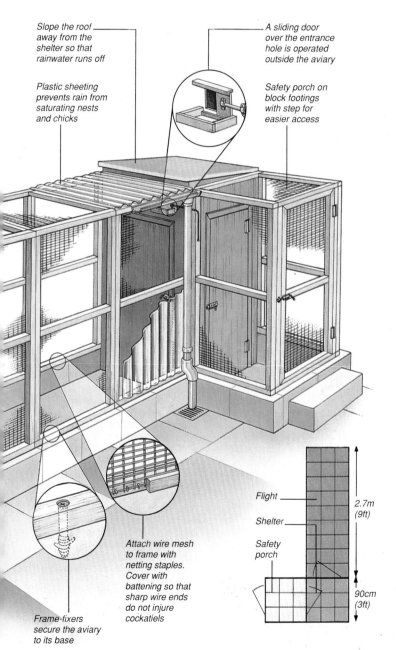

Slope the roof away from the shelter so that rainwater runs off

Plastic sheeting prevents rain from saturating nests and chicks

A sliding door over the entrance hole is operated outside the aviary

Safety porch on block footings with step for easier access

Attach wire mesh to frame with netting staples. Cover with battening so that sharp wire ends do not injure cockatiels

Frame-fixers secure the aviary to its base

Flight

Shelter

Safety porch

2.7m (9ft)

90cm (3ft)

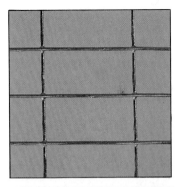

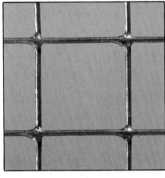

Above left: *2.5x1.25cm (1x0.5in), 19G mesh, an inexpensive option for cockatiel housing.* Above: *2.5x1.25cm (1x0.5in), 16G mesh is thicker and more durable.* Left: *2.5x2.5cm (1x1in) mesh, suitable for indoor use, but mice could gain access to an outside aviary.*

points before placing a firm order and, if possible, try to visit the suppliers nearest to your home, so you can judge their workmanship.

Be sure to have the accurate dimensions of the aviary with you, so you can cost the structure in terms of the number of panels you require. In most cases, especially with a large supplier, the difference between making the panels yourself or buying them ready for assembly will not be very great. When you add in your time, it is probably worthwhile buying at least the flight in kit form.

The safety porch
In addition to the flight panels, you will need extra ones to form the safety porch around the door to the flight. The safety porch ensures that none of your cockatiels escape when you enter the aviary. They are swift fliers and, especially with a group housed together, there is always the possibility that one could slip past you. The principal feature of the porch is its double

doors, which enable you to enter the aviary through the door of the safety porch and to close this behind you before you open the door leading into the aviary itself. Even if it escapes from the aviary, the cockatiel can only fly into the porch, being restricted by the mesh here. You can then drive it back or catch and return it to the flight.

The arrangement of doors on a safety porch will be important. The outer door should open outwards so you can enter easily and have space to put down a cleaning bucket and tools without needing to hold the bucket and squeeze the door shut behind you. For easy access, the door into the flight should open inwards.

Building the aviary
If you decide to make the flight units yourself, stick to a sectional design in which the components can be bolted together and later dismantled and moved if necessary. Choose the right mesh to cover the framework. It should be at least 19 gauge (19G), and preferably even thicker – 16 gauge (16G) is more durable. A mesh size of 2.5x1.25cm(1x0.5in) is suitable. Discount suppliers advertise in the birdkeeping magazines, but you will

need to buy your timber from a local source. You can arrange for all the necessary lengths to be cut to size, which will save you time when assembling the flight. You can obtain timber already treated with a preservative, but check beforehand that this is safe for use with livestock. Although cockatiels are not usually destructive towards woodwork, they may gnaw at exposed pieces.

Of course, the lifespan of the aviary will be significantly increased if the timbers are treated, so the only option is to apply a safe preservative yourself. Several coats may be required and this will undoubtedly prove a time-consuming task. Support the lengths of timber on trestles, with newspaper on the floor beneath to absorb any spillage, and use a broad paintbrush for the preservative. It is easier to treat the timber before making it into frames, but once you have cut the joints, remember to treat the freshly exposed wood surfaces as well. Planed timber is an unnecessary expense; rough timber will blend in just as well in a garden setting. You can also save on cost by opting for timber 3.75cm(1.5in) square, rather than 5cm(2in) square, although the latter will obviously result in a stronger structure.

Working to your plan, be sure to number the panels that will form the flight as each one is completed, thus making it easier to assemble the final structure. One of the most important elements influencing the dimensions will be the width of the wire mesh. Clearly, if you have based the size of the panels on the width of the mesh, this will save time and minimize wastage (see page 26).

Fixing the mesh
Aviary mesh is usually attached with netting staples, applied about every 5cm(2in) or so around the perimeter of the flight panel. The side with the mesh attached to it will form the inner surface of the flight. When you start, position the mesh so that it overlaps all the sides of the framework by at least 1.25cm(0.5in). This enables you to fix it firmly in place with two rows of netting staples, running in parallel and alternating in position. The strain of the mesh is therefore evenly distributed around the timber and the staples are less likely to work loose over a period of time. Before you start, check that the mesh is held square and taut by placing individual staples strategically at each bottom corner. Then carefully unroll the mesh over the face of the frame and tack it tightly in place at the top. With a pair of wire cutters, free the roll by cutting across the strands of mesh in a straight line. Finally, adjust the covering over the frame by pulling the wire at the bottom edge.

Provided you did not drive the netting staples at this end hard into the timber, you should just be able to pull the mesh slightly to make it as taut as possible. Use one hand for this purpose (and wear a glove, otherwise it may be painful) and then, without letting the mesh slip back again, hammer these two netting staples home with your other hand.

Because you have not cut the edges of the mesh they should be quite smooth, but sharp loose ends are inevitable at the top and bottom of the frame and could injure the cockatiels once the aviary is assembled. Using wire clippers, cut these projections back as close as possible to the nearest horizontal strand. Sweep up these offcuts carefully so that other pets do not cut their feet on sharp pieces of wire. And, as a final precaution for the cockatiels, fix a length of hardwood battening over the cut edges of mesh, using panel pins for this purpose as they will be less likely to split the thin wood.

The shelter
Cockatiels are quite hardy, but they do need somewhere dry and sheltered where they can escape from the worst of the weather. Traditionally this has taken the form of a shedlike structure attaching directly to the rear of the flight.

Indeed, if you have a spare shed in your garden, you can convert this for the cockatiels and attach the flight around an outside window, having first removed the glass so the birds can move freely in and out. On the other hand, you may decide to buy a shed rather than build a similar structure. You may well find a bargain at a garden centre in the late autumn or winter, when display models are usually sold off at considerable discounts.

If you decide to construct a shelter unit yourself, build it on a similar sectional basis to the flight. The procedure is somewhat more complicated, however, because you need to allow for the slope of the roof. The simplest design is a flat roof made from tough marine plywood, positioned with its highest point adjoining the flight and sloping away to the rear of the shelter. Rainwater is easily channelled away from here, using guttering connected either to a water-butt or soakaway.

Ensure that the shelter itself is well-lit so the cockatiels will be encouraged to roost here. Incorporate a window at the rear of the shelter, therefore, possibly as part of the entrance door. You can also fit a smaller window into one side of the shelter. Cover both windows with wire mesh, fixed carefully in place with netting staples, and batten down the cut ends, otherwise the cockatiels are likely to fly directly at the glass, and may even kill themselves. Newly fledged chicks are most at risk.

It may be worthwhile insulating the shelter, even to the extent of double-glazing the windows. Units without an expensive surround are relatively cheap. To insulate the walls, use proper household insulation material, which is less of a fire hazard than other materials, such as polystyrene. There is also less risk of mice deciding to set up home here, given the unpleasant nature of the quilting.

Follow the recommended precautions when using insulation quilt and then cover it completely, either with oil-tempered hardboard or, better still, with thin plywood, which is more durable. If you wish, you can paint these coverings with a light emulsion, which will brighten up the interior of the shelter. Finally, it may be worthwhile covering all accessible edges with battening, so the cockatiels are not tempted to nibble at any exposed edges of wood, particularly hardboard, as this will not be very resistant to their beaks.

Although it is possible to carry out some of this work before erecting the shelter, you may prefer to wait until the panels are in position. However, it is certainly easier to insulate the roof unit before the structure is fully assembled, by turning it upside down on a level surface.

Construct the shelter doors separately and only hang them right at the end of the construction process, otherwise they will simply be in the way and may be damaged as a result. A connecting door, opening outwards from the shelter into the flight, is vital, irrespective of any other entrances to the aviary itself. Indeed separate external doors to the shelter and flight are not essential.

If you decide to have just a single entrance, make this door part of the shelter, not forgetting to allow for the surrounding safety porch (see page 30). You can then enter the flight through the connecting door. Because the cockatiels will be fed in the shelter, this is where you will need to have easiest access.

Assembling the components
Aviary building is best carried out when there is a likelihood of dry weather, so spring and summer are usually the most popular seasons. Winter tends to be too cold and you cannot be sure that the freshly mixed concrete in the base has dried out properly if there is a risk of frost and snow.

Try to start early in the day, so that the work is completed by the evening if all runs smoothly. You will need some help to move the various panels into their respective positions and hold them there while

Above: *Use mesh to protect the woodwork of the aviary against the cockatiels' beaks. Provide a variety of wooden perches. The birds will gnaw at the sideshoots.*

the felt being ripped off in a strong wind. The sun can also be harmful, however, and in persistently warm climates you may choose to paint the felt with a suitable exterior paint, preferably white in colour. Some of the sun's heat will then be reflected, thus increasing the lifespan of the felt, which may otherwise split prematurely.

Perches

It is easier to fix the perches in the aviary before the doors are hinged in place. Again, as with a cockatiel kept in the home, check that the branches are quite clean and free from obvious signs of mould, because the cockatiels will almost inevitably strip off the bark.

You can wire the perches in place, relying on the wooden uprights of the flight for support, rather than on the mesh, which is likely to break in time if used to hold the perches firm. Be sure to provide adequate support, otherwise the cockatiels may have difficulty in mating, which can lead to disappointing breeding results.

Provide at least four perches in the aviary – two in the flight and two in the shelter. Set them across the structure, rather than lengthways, to give the cockatiels a larger area of flying space. The birds tend to prefer to roost on the highest perches when they are not breeding, so make sure that the perches in the shelter are positioned above the two in the outside flight. This should encourage the cockatiels to enter the flight and move freely in and out of the shelter.

The entrance hole

You will need to cut a small entry hole, approximately 23cm(9in) square, at a relatively high point on the side of the shelter where it joins the flight. Fix a platform firmly in place here, extending it a short distance, perhaps 15cm(6in) or so, at either side of the entry. As an added refinement to prevent draughts, you can add small vertical sheets of plywood around the sides of the platform.

they are fixed in place. Join the frames together with bolts and washers and keep these well-oiled, so that the structure can be easily dismantled and moved to a new site. Special frame-fixers that pass through the timber into the blocks beneath are useful for securing the aviary to its base. Once the main part of the structure is in place, you can put up the safety porch, and fix the roof panels in place.

The roof of the shelter will need to be protected with roofing felt. Where the roof fits onto the shelter, fill any obvious gaps with a proprietary sealant. Some planing of the timbers along the side of the shelter may also be necessary to ensure a snug fit. Then apply two layers of roofing felt over the whole area, fixing it firmly in place with clout nails and battening around the edges. This will help to prevent

33

Extending the existing aviary

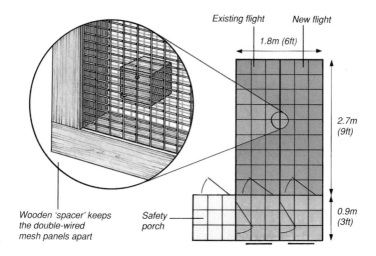

Existing flight   *New flight*

1.8m (6ft)

2.7m (9ft)

0.9m (3ft)

Wooden 'spacer' keeps the double-wired mesh panels apart

Safety porch

You may wish to close the cockatiels in the shelter, either when the weather is very bad, or because you want to catch them. Use a piece of plywood to make a cover for the entrance and slide it between suitable runners placed above and below the hole. Attach a stout single strand of wire to the cover, making sure that it extends outside the aviary mesh. By pulling the wire, you can move the plywood to cover the entrance hole.

Final details
Finally, to finish off the inside of the aviary, add the doors. Fit bolts where appropriate to ensure that a sudden gust of wind will not blow them open and secure all exterior doors with a clasp and padlock to prevent escapes and – possibly more seriously – for security reasons. Several breeders have been burgled, and have lost many birds because their aviaries were not locked in any way. Although insurance cover may be available in some cases, it tends to be relatively expensive for the small-scale birdkeeper and this simple precaution will be a deterrent.

Externally, you can face the blockwork with mortar and then paint it if required. Replace the cut

Above: *Double-wiring is essential in adjoining flights housing cockatiels. It ensures there is a suitable gap between the pairs, so the birds cannot injure each other.*

turves around the flight. It is a good idea to lay a path, or at least to set paving stones in the turves, so that you do not create bare patches in the lawn, by constantly walking back and forth to feed the birds.

Extending the aviary
Any additions to the aviary should be made in the early autumn, after the breeding season, so that there will be no risk of interfering with the cockatiels' nesting activities. You may be able to place a second flight alongside the existing structure, using one of the sides as part of the new unit. It is important to wire the outer face of the panel common to both structures so that there is a gap between flights, otherwise cockatiels in adjoining aviaries may nibble, or even bite the feet of their neighbours, which can result in serious injury.

You must also check that the double-wiring remains intact. After a time, the lengths of mesh often sag slightly on the frame, so that the space between them is

Block of aviary flights for breeding

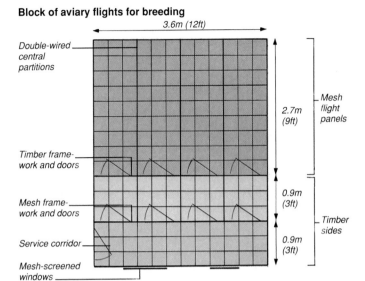

Double-wired central partitions

Timber frame-work and doors

Mesh frame-work and doors

Service corridor

Mesh-screened windows

3.6m (12ft)

2.7m (9ft) — Mesh flight panels

0.9m (3ft) — Timber sides

0.9m (3ft)

Above: *A block of cockatiel flights serviced off a rear corridor. The shedlike structure also includes the birds' roosting quarters. A safety porch is unnecessary in this case.*

reduced, making it easier for neighbouring cockatiels to have direct contact. Once the aviaries are assembled, it will obviously be difficult to rectify this problem, but the simplest way of dealing with it is to cut short lengths of battening, and fit these through the mesh. You could even hold them in place with netting staples, although usually the pressure of the mesh alone holds them in place, while they serve to keep the strands apart. If the cockatiels nibble them away, you will need to replace these 'spacers' at regular intervals.

Breeders with large numbers of cockatiels often arrange a number of flights in blocks, servicing them from a single corridor that runs the full length of the flights. With this design there is no need for a safety porch, as the outer door to the corridor serves the purpose. Having closed this door, you can then safely enter the individual flights. Should a cockatiel fly out, it will simply remain trapped in the corridor and can be returned to its

flight. The aviary shelters form part of the building in which the corridor is situated, so the indoor quarters are often made of a mesh framework, rather like the flight, instead of having solid walls.

Introducing the birds

Make all your preparations in advance, fixing the food and water containers in place and laying clean newspapers down on the floor of the shelter. Tape the sheets together so that they are not disturbed by the cockatiels. Release birds into a new aviary during the late morning, preferably over a weekend or similar period when you will be at home and can watch their progress. You may decide to confine them in the shelter for a day or two, so that they become used to feeding here. In any event, place the cockatiels in the shelter at first and allow them to find their own way out. They should return inside to roost at night.

It is vital to supervise the cockatiels at this stage. The vast majority of birds, especially older stock, will settle in rapidly and soon find their way around their new surroundings, but young, recently-fledged cockatiels can be more of a problem. If they have shown no

Above: *This is a view of flights running off a central service corridor, with a heater at one end.*

sign of wanting to eat and drink by the second day, close them in the shelter. This alone may be sufficient to rekindle their appetite, provided the birds are otherwise healthy. Should you be in any doubt, contact your veterinarian without delay.

After this initial stage, things should run quite smoothly. You will need to check the cockatiels regularly each day, however, to ensure that they are not ill or injured. They will need food and fresh water on a daily basis, especially if you are offering perishable greenfood. During the breeding season, the birds may well require two feeds every day, morning and afternoon. On each occasion, pause to look at the cockatiels for a few moments. When you have been doing this regularly for a few months, you will soon notice if any birds appear even slightly off colour.

Vermin
One major problem that you may have to face is the appearance of rodents in or around the aviary. At worst, rats are capable of killing

cockatiels, as well as scaring them so much that they neglect their chicks. The appearance of small mountains of earth and longish, brown pelleted droppings are an indication of their presence. Eliminate rats without delay; where poisoning is not practical, perhaps because there are young children around, seek the help of a pest control officer.

Mice can also become serious pests, increasing rapidly in number where food is freely available. This is not surprising, when calculations suggest that a single pair can produce over one hundred young mice during a year. Several mice can destroy an aviary quite rapidly, especially if they get behind the lining material on the walls of the shelter. At the very least, you will need to pull off the lining and clean behind it, which is an unpleasant task, even when the mice have been removed. Feeding cockatiels in the shelter means that seed will be less accessible to the smaller rodents which, when young, can squeeze through most aviary wire. Once inside, they may decide to nest in the floor, and here you will not be able to use traditional methods of control, such as poisoning and killer traps, in case the cockatiel can reach them.

However, it may be possible to place a killer trap safely in the cockatiels' quarters, provided you position it in the centre of a parrot cage, the door of which is securely closed. The mice will be able to move in and out between the bars of the cage, thus reaching the trap, whereas the cockatiels will be kept outside. Killer traps only take one mouse at a setting and the box traps that catch mice alive are more efficient at eliminating greater numbers. They can catch well over a dozen mice during the course of a night and have no dangerous components, so you can use them quite safely within an aviary.

It will take the mice several days to become used to a live trap, which consists of two parts, a base and a lid. Bait the trap with the lid off for the first few days, until the mice are feeding regularly here. Once the lid is in place, the mice can still enter easily, but they cannot escape and so remain trapped in the box.

Aviaries and cats

Although a keen mouser will kill any mice that stray outside the aviary, there is clearly no possibility of introducing a cat in with the cockatiels to catch mice. You could shut the cockatiels in the flight or remove them temporarily from the aviary, so giving your cat free access. This can help to eliminate a mouse population.

At other times, cats can be troublesome around an aviary,

especially when the cockatiels are breeding. They may climb up the mesh onto the roof of the aviary and try to reach the birds from above. This can lead to the loss of eggs and chicks, if the cockatiels are disturbed as a result.

Strangely enough, when you keep a cat yourself, you are less likely to have problems with cats around the aviary. It is largely a matter of territories – your cat stays within your garden and so other cats are less likely to come in. Although kittens, in particular, may be troublesome, an older cat soon realizes that it will not be able to catch the cockatiels, and so ignores them.

If you are plagued with cats, however, you will need to protect the aviary. This is quite easily done by stringing thin strands of wire on short poles around the top of the aviary. You can also add another layer of mesh on the top wooden part of the roof frame. Use thin 22 gauge (22G) mesh, 5x2.5cm(2x1in) in size tacked in place with staples.

The wire around the sides of the aviary will make it difficult for the cats to climb onto the roof section. Any that do overcome this barrier will find it hard to walk over the thin mesh. With both obstructions in place, the vast majority of cats will be deterred from disturbing the cockatiels. If you do not incorporate these features into the original plan, remove the birds while modifications are carried out, as the work is bound to disturb them.

Protecting the aviary from cats

Deter cats from climbing onto an aviary, particularly when there are chicks in the nest

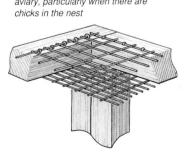

Feeding

One reason for the cockatiel's early popularity is that it can exist largely on a diet of dry seed and water. However, during recent years, cockatiels' nutritional needs have been properly studied and it is now clear that if you want to keep your birds in top condition and achieve the best breeding results, then you must offer them a much wider range of foodstuffs.

Cereal seeds

Seeds, like all foodstuffs, contain carbohydrate, fat and protein. Certain vitamins and minerals may also be present, as well as a variable percentage of water. In the wild, cockatiels forage largely on the ground, seeking grass seeds as a major part of their diet. These seeds contain a relatively high proportion of carbohydrate and correspondingly lower levels of fat and protein. Similarly, pet and aviary cockatiels are usually offered a seed mixture containing

Below and right: *Offer a varied diet that includes seeds, fresh foods and food supplements.*

mainly plain canary seed and a variety of millets – small, round seeds varying in colour from pale yellow to red.

Groats, the dehusked form of oats, are a more specialist seed, belonging to the cereal group. They are relatively easy to digest and so are popular during the breeding season when there are young chicks in the nest. Groats can also be valuable for weaning purposes, when the young cockatiels are first separated from their parents. However, these cereal seeds do not offer a complete, balanced diet for cockatiels and other foods are essential to compensate for vitamin and protein deficiencies.

Oil-based seeds

Most seed mixes for cockatiels include a limited proportion of sunflower seed. Sunflower is an oil-based seed, rich in fat, low in carbo-hydrate, and a valuable source of protein, containing a good range of essential amino-acids.

You may wish to add other ingredients to a standard seed mixture. Hemp is a round, brownish

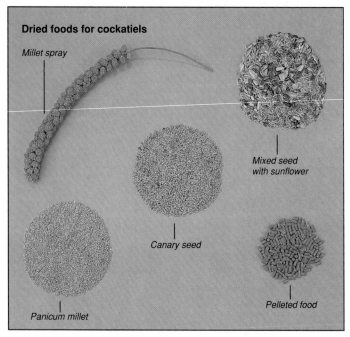

Dried foods for cockatiels

Millet spray

Mixed seed with sunflower

Canary seed

Panicum millet

Pelleted food

seed, traditionally fed during the winter months, because its oil content and high level of minerals are thought to help the cockatiels combat low temperatures. It is not usually fed in any quantity through the warmer months, as then it may lead to obesity.

A balanced diet

Both cereal and oil-based seeds contain proteins, which are made up of individual amino-acid residues. Some of these are recognized as 'essential' because they cannot be manufactured in the body and must be supplied via the cockatiels' food. Although the protein level of a seed may be high, this does not necessarily mean that all the amino-acids are present in adequate quantities. Therefore, it is important to be aware of the value of individual amino-acids.

The amino-acid lysine has been shown to be vital, especially for breeding cockatiels. According to studies carried out at the University of California, chicks receiving a diet deficient in lysine fail to thrive, and often die. Lysine is also known to

be important for feather pigmentation in some parrots, and any dietary shortage can, therefore, be detected easily in them, but this does not apply to cockatiels. However, there are various ways of ensuring that your cockatiels do not suffer from a lysine deficiency and that they also receive other valuable nutritional ingredients.

Individual amino-acids are usually available from your veterinarian, but they are expensive and it is not necessary to resort to this method. During recent years, there has been a rapid expansion in the range of food additives available for birds. You can now obtain balanced supplements in the form of powders that contain a full range of amino-acids, including lysine, as well as vitamins and minerals. Check the labelling if you are unsure, however, because the more traditional brands still offer simply a vitamin and mineral powder and are often cheaper.

Although you can sprinkle the recommended daily dose of powder over the cockatiel's seed,

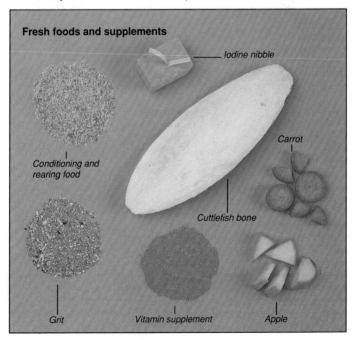

Fresh foods and supplements

Iodine nibble

Conditioning and rearing food

Carrot

Cuttlefish bone

Grit

Vitamin supplement

Apple

this is rather wasteful and ineffective. Cockatiels dehusk seed to obtain the inner kernel and any powder sticking to the seed will probably be discarded. A much more efficient way of offering the supplement is to mix it with fresh foods that have moist surfaces and are eaten in their entirety.

Pelleted foods

It is worthwhile obtaining one of the brands of pelleted food now on the market for cockatiels and other parrotlike birds, because these provide a relatively balanced and complete diet on their own.

Introduce the pellets alongside the normal seed mix and, hopefully, the cockatiels will soon start to eat them as part of their daily diet. Once this point is reached, you can increase the relative proportion of pellets on offer and cut back on the seed. Some ranges offer a maintenance diet and also a breeder's ration, with a higher level of protein. By changing from one to the other in the spring, you will ensure that your cockatiels receive the best possible diet for the forthcoming breeding season. Because pellets are very dry, however, they will stimulate the cockatiel's thirst and you may have to add an extra drinker to ensure

that their water supply does not run out. This could be harmful and may result in kidney damage, even over a short period.

Buying and storing seed

You can buy the various ingredients for a cockatiel seed mixture either separately, or ready-mixed. Find a reputable seed supplier, because poor quality seed is likely to be harmful for the cockatiels, certainly over a period of time. Choose a pet shop with a fairly rapid turnover, so that you do not purchase old seed. Seed that has been stored has a lower vitamin content than freshly gathered seed. It is impossible to assess the nutritional value of seed simply by looking at it, but you can conduct a simple germination test at home. Immerse a sample in warm water and leave it to stand for a day or so. Then drain off the water, and place the seeds on damp towelling in a warm spot. If the seed is reasonably fresh, then a high percentage of the seeds in this trial sample should sprout.

Below: *Millet sprays are extremely popular with cockatiels. They can be fed dry or soaked, which makes them an easily digested and valuable food for young chicks.*

Above: *Cockatiels often prefer greenstuff to fruit, but few will resist a slice of sweet apple. Wash all fresh foods thoroughly first.*

You may be able to negotiate a discount if you are buying seed in quantity from a pet shop but, again, do not be tempted to overstock. Aim to store no more than you need for three months. Keep the seed dry and out of the reach of rodents. A metal dustbin is most suitable for this purpose and you can fill a small tin each day and use a scoop to feed the cockatiels.

Seed that has not been thoroughly cleaned can be very dusty and may contain debris, such as stones. It may well prove dangerous for the cockatiels, especially if it has not been dried properly after harvesting, because deadly fungi will have been allowed to develop. Perhaps even more lethal is seed contaminated by rodent droppings and urine. This can spread various diseases to your cockatiels, often resulting in a high mortality rate.

Empty and clean out the storage bin before adding new seed, so there is less likelihood of fodder mites becoming established here. With the naked eye, you may just be able to see these minute creatures moving among the seed, or they may show up more clearly against a darker background at the bottom of the bin. There may be a sweet, sickly smell associated with them. While there is no clear evidence to show that they are harmful, they obviously will not improve the quality of the seed.

Soaking seed

Adding water to seed triggers the process of germination and various chemical changes take place within the kernel. Vitamin B levels increase and the protein value also rises. In addition, the hard seed kernel is softened, making it more digestible. For all these reasons, many breeders use soaked seed when there are young cockatiels in the nest.

Millet sprays are very popular and easily prepared. Simply immerse one or two sprays for each pair of cockatiels in a bowl of warm water for a day, then remove them and wash them thoroughly under running water from the tap, transferring them to a colander if necessary. The cockatiels normally accept the soaked millet greedily, eating all the kernels after a few hours, but always remove the sprays after a day, otherwise they are likely to turn mouldy and can threaten the cockatiels' health.

Even after the young cockatiels have left the nest, soaked millet sprays make a useful weaning food. Attach them close to the perch with a peg, or twist the stem around a netting staple specially positioned for this purpose.

Greenfood

Cockatiels also benefit from a regular supply of greenfood. This is a valuable source of Vitamin A, which is usually deficient in seed. (Vitamin A deficiency is often implicated in outbreaks of candidiasis, see page 49.) As with soaked millet sprays, the birds will consume larger quantities when there are chicks in the nest, but greenfood is beneficial if fed in appropriately smaller amounts throughout the year.

Chickweed (*Stellaria media*) is very popular with cockatiels, and grows quite easily throughout much of the year. During prolonged periods of dry sunny weather, it may become rather leggy, compared with the more compact,

green shoots favoured by the cockatiels. Generally speaking, gardeners do not encourage chickweed, but it is worth cultivating some in a shaded area, where it can be kept watered. This should ensure a regular supply from spring to autumn and possibly beyond, in mild weather. Seeds are available from seed merchants who offer wild as well as cultivated flowers on their lists for gardeners.

You can, of course, gather chickweed where it grows wild, but there is always a possibility that it may have been contaminated with chemicals of various types. By using garden supplies only, you should be able to ensure that it is safe, as well as fresh. Always wash all greenfoods, however, in case they have been soiled by animals.

As autumn approaches, you may have plantain (*Plantago sp.*) seedheads on your lawn. Seeding grasses, especially meadow grass (*Poa annua*), are another valuable greenfood. They are popular with cockatiels, but do not use them if

Above: *Try to offer some greenfood two or three times a week all year and daily during the breeding period. You may be able to grow your own regular supply.*

you have treated your lawn with a weed-killing preparation in the past months. Many chemicals leave residues for a period of time; if in doubt, check the packaging.

Of the garden vegetables, perpetual spinach (*Beta vulgaris*) is probably the most suitable for cockatiels, because even during the winter you can usually obtain small quantities. It is also very easy to grow from seed. Cockatiels often prefer the thin-stalked, young leaves, rather than the larger, coarse stems. It may be worthwhile chopping spinach leaves into small pieces; otherwise, even if you offer them in a feeding pot, the birds tend to pull them onto the floor and they become dirty as a result.

Another useful fresh food item during the winter months is carrot, also rich in Vitamin A. Scrub or peel the skin, and then dice the carrot into small pieces. Cockatiels usually prefer greenstuff to fruit, but most will take sweet dessert apples – again washed and cut up to prevent wastage. A few cockatiels may also sample grapes, but not if other fresh foods are available.

Be sure to remove any uneaten fresh foods, as wilted, soiled greenstuff and fruit are likely to be harmful to the cockatiel's digestive system. Many breeders offer fresh foods in the morning, removing any surplus late in the afternoon. This is a good time to offer soaked millet spray, which in turn is taken out the following morning. In this way, the chicks should have a supply of seed in their crops overnight, and the adult cockatiels will prefer the soaked millet sprays to dry seed, so wastage is minimal. Of course, a seed mixture and fresh drinking water must always be available.

Below: *A selection of greenfoods often fed to cockatiels. Some can be grown on a windowsill indoors.*

Other rearing foods

When there are chicks in the nest, some cockatiel breeders offer their birds a regular supply of wholemeal bread soaked in an equal mix of milk and water. It is absolutely essential that such a mixture is fresh and that there is no likelihood of the milk souring, which tends to make bread and milk an unsatisfactory option in warm climates. There is also some dispute concerning the cockatiel's ability to break down the milk sugar; it may be that it gives rise to digestive upsets.

A much better option is to provide a softbill food. This may already be available to the cockatiels if they are housed in the company of softbills of any kind. (Softbills do not eat seed but rely on 'soft' foods, and those suitable for keeping with cockatiels include zosterops and fruit doves.) There are various brands of softbill food on the market, some of which can be offered straight from the packet, whereas others need mixing with

Suitable greenfoods

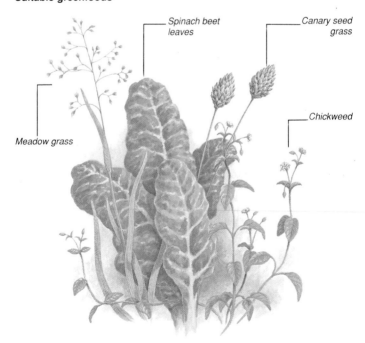

Spinach beet leaves

Canary seed grass

Chickweed

Meadow grass

water. Cockatiels normally eat softbill food quite readily, especially during the breeding period, and it provides a valuable source of essential amino-acids. Offer a small quantity regularly before the start of the breeding season, so that the birds have an opportunity to sample it. Canary rearing foods are also suitable but, again, make sure that they do not turn sour.

There may well be occasions, especially with a large number of chicks in a nest, when you will need to supplement the parents' feeding activities, or even remove chicks for hand-raising if they are to survive (see page 54). Special hand-rearing diets, recently introduced onto the market, are ideal for cockatiels. Critical elements, such as the lysine level, can be accurately controlled in such products, specifically formulated for this purpose. Mix a fresh batch for the chicks at each feed. Ensure that it is warm, but not too hot, which will scald the chicks, nor too cold. Test a little of the mixture on the back of your hand before using it. Young chicks require a fairly liquid food, thoroughly mixed and with no lumps. If you cannot obtain a branded rearing food, you will have to resort to a combination of baby foods from your local pharmacy or supermarket, but results may be less reliable. Again, mix them with water to ensure that the food is adequately diluted. This is particularly important during the first few days, when the chicks should receive a high fluid diet.

Cuttlefish bone, grit and iodine
Cuttlefish bone is a vital part of the diet of adult cockatiels, especially during the breeding season, when the birds will consume more cuttlefish bone because its main ingredient, calcium, is vital for sound eggshells. (Seed is notably low in this important mineral.) Cuttlefish can also be given to hand-reared youngsters from about three weeks onwards; simply scrape some of the bone over their food using a sharp knife.

Above: *Cuttlefish bone is a valuable source of calcium and other minerals. Hold it in place using one of the special clips available from pet stores. The birds nibble at the powdery side.*

Cuttlefish bones (not bones as such, but buoyancy 'chambers' for marine molluscs) are sometimes washed up on beaches, especially after a storm. Provided they are not contaminated with tar, you can use them for cockatiels, but first wash them thoroughly. To do this, stand them in a bucket of fresh water and change this twice daily over the course of a week. Scrub the bones with a clean scrubbing brush, and after a final rinse, leave them to dry off completely. Then store them in a clean plastic bag for later use.

Cuttlefish bone is also available from pet shops. Broken bones cost less and are just as acceptable to the cockatiels. Special clips to hold cuttlefish bone are useful, although you may need to break whole bones into smaller pieces. Cockatiels often perch on the bones and may soil them with droppings. Budgerigar grit, usually available in packeted form, is equally suitable for cockatiels and, like cuttlefish bone, should always be on offer to the birds. It can provide valuable minerals, and oystershell, in particular, dissolves quite readily in the cockatiel's digestive system, compared with relatively insoluble mineralized grit. Provide grit in a small 'hook-on' container topped up each week, so that a constant supply of particles of different sizes is available.

A supply of grit ensures that seed kernels can be ground down effectively in the gizzard because, of course, cockatiels have no teeth to perform this task. Many breeders like to offer a mixture of oystershell and mineralized grits, because of their varied mineral content.

Pet shops also sell iodine blocks that you simply fix in place in the cage or aviary. They provide the iodine required by the thyroid glands in the neck that influence the cockatiel's metabolism and overall level of activity. Seed is also often low in iodine.

Food pots and drinkers

Most cages are already equipped with feeders and drinkers. Although open pots are suitable for seed, they are less than ideal for water, because seed husks – and even droppings – are likely to contaminate the water supply and can represent a health hazard for the cockatiel. Tubular drinkers of various designs are more suitable and widely available, but check the fittings to ensure that you can attach the drinker to the cage.

In aviary surroundings, seed is usually provided in hoppers, rather

Below: *A suspended bowl-shaped seed feeder. The birds perch on the rim when feeding; some seed scattering is unavoidable.*

than in open pots. Obtain a plastic base that fits over a jam jar. When inverted, the jar becomes a reservoir for the seed, which is dispensed via the base. These feeders cannot be attached to the mesh, however, so you must either stand them on the floor or on a secure feeding shelf. (This is easy to make by using brackets to secure a suitably sized piece of plywood to the side of the shelter). Some designs of hopper will not dispense sunflower seed, however, so you would have to offer sunflower separately from the smaller cereal seeds.

When feeding cockatiels from open pots, position the containers alongside perches. This prevents spillage of seed, as the birds do not need to fly on and off the rim of the container to feed.

Even if there is no aviary mesh in this part of the shelter, you can still fix a hook-on container in place. Mark the position of the hooks and drive two netting staples into the corresponding places. Provided that you do not hammer these too far into the woodwork, you will have two ready-made supports to accommodate the hooks of the food pot.

Offer perishable foods of any kind separately from dried seed and wash these pots thoroughly after each feed, taking care to rinse them properly after using a detergent. Although you can obtain special racks to hold greenfood, these are not very effective because the cockatiels usually pull the stalks out all over the floor.

If you find that the cockatiels are spilling large amounts of seed, you may want to invest in a winnower to reclaim the seed. This machine separates seeds from husks and other debris, although not all designs can cope with sunflower seed. In any event, try to position the food pots so that dry seed is confined to one area and fresh perishable foods are offered elsewhere in the shelter. This will make it easier to collect good seed, but discard any that is damp or contaminated with droppings.

Health care

Cockatiels are usually hardy, long-lived birds and rarely prone to illness. With sensible management, they should live well into their twenties. You are most likely to encounter health problems with newly acquired stock, rather than with birds that are well established in their quarters (see page 11). By keeping recent acquisitions on their own for about a fortnight, you have an opportunity to ensure that they are healthy, and you can treat them for parasites before adding them to a colony aviary. Do not be tempted to introduce new cockatiels to an established group during the breeding season, because this will be disruptive, leading to the loss of both eggs and chicks.

Parasites

Diseases caused by parasites are often seen in cockatiels and yet are easily prevented. Parasites can be broadly divided into two groups: those that live externally on the cockatiel's body; and those that are found within the body. In the external group, various mites – and even sometimes lice – can be associated with cockatiels and are usually most prevalent in the breeding season.

Red mites live within the nestbox and emerge from crevices to feed on the cockatiel's blood, which gives this parasite its characteristic colour. Wild birds attracted to the aviary roof can introduce red mites as they preen themselves, but you can protect your stock by covering most of the roof of the flight with translucent plastic. (This also enables the cockatiels to perch outside with some protection from the elements throughout the year.) In any event, be sure to treat all cockatiels with a safe aerosol spray marketed for this purpose.

At the end of the breeding season, remove the nestbox and wash it thoroughly in a solution that will kill these avian parasites. Again, such products are available from pet shops. A population of red mites can grow very quickly under favourable conditions, and they are capable of surviving from one year to the next without feeding. A severe infestation will cause considerable feather irritation and may lead adult birds to pluck their young. Chicks are also at risk from anaemia caused by the mites' feeding habits.

Roundworms are perhaps even more significant in terms of a cockatiel's health. The nature of the life cycle of these internal parasites poses a potentially dangerous threat to the birds. Roundworm eggs are voided in the cockatiel's droppings and millions can rapidly accumulate in the environment. They soon become infective and can start the cycle again. For example, if a cockatiel eats a piece of greenfood contaminated with droppings containing mature roundworm eggs, further roundworms will develop in the bird's gut. Thorough cleaning of the cockatiel's quarters is essential to prevent such reinfection occurring.

The eggs thrive in dark, moist surroundings and may remain viable for years. On a soil floor, earthworms may also ingest the parasitic eggs, and introduce them to a neighbouring flight as part of a worm cast. Obviously, once you have a parasitic problem of this type, it will be difficult to resolve without a considerable amount of effort. As well as taking sensible

Below: *Treat a newly acquired bird for possible mites. Use treatments specially formulated for birds and follow all the instructions.*

Life cycles of parasites

Direct life cycles

Disease can be introduced by new infected birds; earthworms via worm casts; and on contaminated shoes

Other factors that play a part in the life cycle

Infection spreads quickly in a flight difficult to clean. Birds that feed on the ground ingest many worm eggs

Foods pots soiled by droppings, and the grass under perches are common routes of infection. Worm eggs can survive for months and are hard to eliminate

Indirect life cycles

The cockatiel can only become infected by eating an invertebrate containing an immature tapeworm

Here, parasites are spread indirectly via tapeworm eggs passed out from the gut in segments, callled proglottids

Beetles and woodlice eat the eggs. Only then will the tapeworm start to develop from the egg – a vital stage

Once outside the bird, the proglottids containing eggs will rupture. The eggs then spread through the aviary

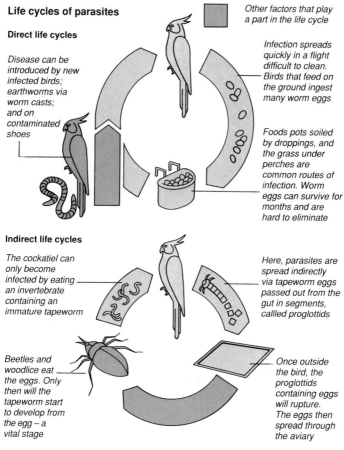

Above: *Cockatiels are susceptible to parasitic worm infections, which can spread from aviary to aviary.*

precautions to ensure that such parasites do not gain access to the aviary, you should always deworm all cockatiels properly before releasing them into your collection.

Do not simply accept that they may have been dewormed at an earlier stage. This may be true, but there is certainly no guarantee that they received an adequate dose of treatment and they could still be infected. Seek the advice of an avian veterinarian for medication. Although some preparations can simply be added to the drinking water, these are less effective than those given to each individual bird. Of course, it is possible to test for the presence of parasitic worm eggs in the cockatiel's droppings and, again, this can be carried out by a veterinarian. The symptoms of

a roundworm infection are surprisingly varied. Some cockatiels show little adverse reaction, whereas others lose weight and appear generally sickly and dull. Death can be quite common, especially among young birds, so no breeder can afford to ignore this potential problem. With a pet cockatiel, regular treatment is less likely to be necessary, as the bird is living in isolation.

Tapeworms are far less significant than roundworms, because they do not usually have a direct life cycle. Cockatiels only become infected if they consume a woodlouse, or

some other invertebrate that is already carrying an immature tapeworm in its body. This is unlikely, but if a tapeworm infection is diagnosed, treatment by injection rather than tablet is quite feasible.

Giardia is a microscopic intestinal parasite related to the amoeba, and it is one of the most frequent causes of diarrhoea in cockatiels. Interestingly, it appears to be far more common in North America than in Europe, for reasons which are not understood at present. The resulting diarrhoea tends to be rather mucoid, forming strands as it is voided from the body, and usually has a highly unpleasant odour. Diagnosis depends on examining faecal samples, and treatment with a drug called dimetridazole is possible. The droppings are infectious, so strict hygienic measures are essential to prevent the disease spreading.

Another group of similar parasites is found in the blood and can occasionally be isolated in cockatiels. These protozoa can be transmitted from bird to bird by red mites. They may not cause any harm, although they can lead to heart failure, if they invade this muscle. It should be possible to recognize their presence in a blood smear, although relatively little is known about them. (See page 46 for details of mite control.)

Above: *An infrared lamp provides a valuable source of heat for a sick bird. Secure it with clips.*

Bacterial diseases
A number of bacteria can cause serious disturbances in cockatiels, especially when the birds are kept in dirty surroundings and their food is contaminated. For example, *Escherichia coli* can be introduced from your own hands when you prepare fresh foods. This can give rise to diarrhoea and may spread from the gut throughout the bird's body, with fatal consequences. Always wash your hands, before preparing food for cockatiels.

Treating a sick bird
Accurate diagnosis of illness in cockatiels can be very difficult without laboratory assistance, but you will soon see that a bird is sick. It will sit quietly, with its plumage no longer sleek, and its eyes may be closed. The droppings will alter in appearance and, in some cases, can even show traces of blood.

If you begin treatment during the early stages of the illness, there is a good possibility that the bird will make a full recovery. Antibiotic drugs, prescribed by a veterinarian if necessary, can be administered via the cockatiel's drinking water or, in more acute cases, injected directly by a veterinarian. Carefully follow all instructions about dosage and never stop a course of treatment before the recommended time. Antibiotics are useful in countering bacterial disease, but are of little direct value in viral and most fungal infections. Fortunately, viral infections are uncommon in cockatiels and the main problem involving fungi is candidiasis, which can be controlled by feeding a well-balanced diet.

As well as administering medication, there is much that you can do in terms of nursing to help a cockatiel's recovery. Sick birds need a warm environment – up to 32°C(90°F). You can create this in a hospital cage or, preferably, with an infrared lamp. Choose a 'dull emitter' variety, because this produces heat but not light. Suspend the lamp over part of the cage and the cockatiel will then be able to adjust its position, moving closer to the heat source as necessary. Make sure that water is freely available; a sick cockatiel will find it easier to drink from an open hook-on container, rather than from a tubular drinker. Put food within easy reach; sick birds can sometimes be persuaded to feed from the hand, but do not cause them stress at any stage.

As the cockatiel's condition improves, you can gradually lower the temperature of its surroundings. Before returning a bird to an outside aviary, make sure that it is fully recovered and re-acclimatized. If a cockatiel falls sick through the winter months, it may be necessary to keep it indoors until the spring, when the weather will be warmer.

Egg-binding
Cockatiels are prolific birds and hens may attempt to nest during the colder months of the year, which puts them at increased risk from egg-binding. This serious condition can be rapidly fatal, and affects hens that are about to lay or are already laying. The signs are reasonably specific; an affected bird will leave the nestbox, appearing unsteady on her feet, and may very soon be confined to the floor of the aviary.

A bird in this condition must be handled very gently, so as not to break the egg. The most effective treatment is usually an injection of calcium, given by a veterinarian. This appears to restore the muscular activity, so that the hen can lay the egg without difficulty. In extreme cases, you may need to manipulate the egg very gently out of the body by hand, using a suitable lubricant, such as olive oil, applied to the hen's vent.

Your veterinarian may undertake surgery as a last resort. Even after surgery, hens can make a full recovery and lay again normally in the future, but be sure to prevent them from breeding until the following year. Check the cockatiels' diet after a case of egg-binding. It may be that insufficient cuttlefish bone was available to them, or perhaps they could benefit from a supplement containing Vitamin D_3, which is responsible for moving calcium stores around the body. Cockatiels housed indoors may be deficient in this vitamin, which is normally produced by the action of sunlight on the plumage.

Candidiasis
Another breeding problem linked in part to a vitamin deficiency is candidiasis. It is caused by a yeastlike micro-organism, *Candida albicans*, that tends to flourish when the body is deficient in Vitamin A. 'Cheesy' growths appear in the mouth and throat and may well spread further down the digestive tract. Symptoms are rare in adult cockatiels, and so you may not realize a problem exists until the infection is passed to the chicks during feeding. Since chicks lack effective immunity, *Candida* spreads rapidly through their system and can be the cause of quite heavy mortality in newly hatched birds. Visual diagnosis can be difficult under these circumstances, but if you find that young chicks are dying in large numbers, ask your veterinarian for advice on testing for candidiasis.

Hand-reared chicks can also become infected, especially if they are being fed by a tube that damages the lining of their throat, enabling *Candida* to colonize the damaged tissue. Specific antibiotic treatment can be of value, together with a supplement containing Vitamin A. Offering foods rich in this vitamin, such as greenstuff and carrots, should protect young chicks from the outset.

Feather plucking

This is a relatively common problem in young lutino cockatiels, and usually occurs just as the birds are beginning to feather up. One or both parent birds may be responsible for feather plucking, directing their attention first to the back of the neck, but sometimes removing the feathers over a much wider area of the body.

It may be that the adult cockatiels are keen to breed again and attempt to drive their first-round youngsters from the nestbox by removing their feathers. The youngsters are mutilated very quickly – often within a few hours – so that it is difficult to take effective action. To some extent the condition may be inherited, and there is little that can be done to correct it. However, if you have a pair of cockatiels that you know from previous experience are feather-pluckers, you can take steps to prevent a recurrence of the problem. You could try sprinkling powdered aloes around the necks of the chicks every day as they begin to feather up. The bitter taste of the aloes will, hopefully, deter the adult birds should they start to remove the feathers from their youngsters. Another possibility is to leave a second nestbox in the flight, in the hope that the breeding pair will use it for their second round of eggs, rather than persecute their existing offspring.

Once they leave the nestbox, the young cockatiels will grow new feathers in the course of the next few weeks, and become identical in appearance to their fellows. There is rarely any recurrence of feather plucking once the birds have finallyleft the nest.

Adult cockatiels, unlike cockatoos, rarely pluck their own feathers. An interesting observation from the United States suggests that birds that pluck themselves are infected with the *Giardia* parasite, which appears to trigger a severe skin irritation. In these cases, successful treatment of giardiasis can directly resolve the problem of feather plucking.

First-aid

Because of their rapid flight, cockatiels can seriously injure themselves if they collide with an obstruction, such as a sheet of glass. There is little that you can do with a concussed cockatiel, apart from placing it in a darkened environment, such as a travelling box, and leaving it alone in the hope that it will recover. Obviously, if the cockatiel has fractured its skull in the collision, then the chances of recovery are doubtful.

Fractures of the wing and leg occasionally occur, although they are not common. The affected limb may show an obvious swelling at the site of the fracture, and the cockatiel will be clearly handicapped as a result. Seek the advice of an experienced avian veterinarian about splinting. Avian fractures heal within a few weeks if they are properly supported, although the bird may suffer some accompanying loss of function in the limb concerned. Cockatiels usually adjust well under these circumstances, and their breeding capacity may remain unaffected.

Claw clipping

Overgrown claws can cause a cockatiel to become caught up in its cage or aviary, and so they will need to be trimmed back regularly, perhaps every two months or so. Make sure that the claws really do need clipping, however, by comparing them with those of other cockatiels. Once you start cutting the claws, you may have to continue doing so for the remainder of the bird's life.

Use a sharp pair of clippers for the task and work in a good light, so that you can locate the blood supply, visible as a dark streak running a short distance from the toe down each claw. It will be much easier to identify the blood supply in a lutino bird with pale claws than in a normal cockatiel, which has dark coloured claws.

Clip the claw a short distance beyond the point where the blood supply disappears, so that you do not cause any bleeding. If you do inadvertently cut the claw too short,

dip the foot in a cold solution of potash alum, to encourage clotting. This solution can also be useful for stopping minor bleeding elsewhere on the body – from the cere, for example. Simply immerse some cotton wool in the solution and apply it to the site of the injury.

Below: *A cockatiel's claws rarely require clipping, but if they do become overgrown the bird can get caught up in the aviary mesh.*

Breeding

Unlike many parrots, adult cockatiels can be sexed visually, so that in most cases it is not difficult to recognize a pair. Even with lutinos, the characteristic barring on the tail of hens is still present, although it is harder to recognize from a distance. You may need to catch the cockatiel so that you can examine it in your hand (see page 12). The true albino form of the cockatiel, which is rare, is much harder to sex, however, because no colour pigment of any kind is present in its plumage. You should be able to identify albino cock birds by their song, although they can be surgically sexed by a veterinarian if required. The technique involves the direct inspection of the internal sex organs, via a small incision made in the left flank, while the bird is anaesthetized. It is normally a very safe procedure, from which the cockatiel rapidly recovers.

Surgical sexing can only be carried out reliably on mature cockatiels; with young birds, you may need to resort to the laboratory method of chromosomal karyotyping. This entails studying the specific pair of sex chromosomes to determine the bird's gender. A small sample of blood taken from a plucked feather is used for this purpose.

Early breeding

Cockatiels may be mature at only six months old, but they should be prevented from breeding until their second year. At this stage, there is less risk of young hens becoming egg-bound as a result of their immaturity, and overall fertility is likely to be improved.

Nestboxes

In the late spring, once the weather is mild and sudden cold spells are unlikely, you can hang the nestbox in the flight. Suitable nestboxes are often available from pet shops or specialist suppliers. Alternatively, they are quite simple to build, using timber about 2.5cm(1in) thick. Exterior grade plywood is also quite satisfactory for this purpose.

A nestbox for a pair of cockatiels should measure about 23cm(9in) square and 30cm(12in) deep and have a removable roof section. Incorporate a hinged inspection panel into one of the sides, about 7.5cm(3in) from the base of the box. Without this, it can be very difficult to see into the nestbox once it is fixed up in the aviary.

Most ready-built nestboxes have round access holes for the cockatiels, but if you are building the box yourself it is easier and equally satisfactory to cut a square hole, not exceeding 6.5cm(2.5in) across. A dowelling perch attached to the front of the nestbox, about 2.5cm(1in) below the entrance hole, will facilitate the cockatiels' entry. Some breeders fix a budgerigar ladder inside the nestbox, leading down from the entrance hole, so that the birds can move in and out more easily. Use netting staples to hold the ladder securely in place; if it collapses, it will block off the base of the nestbox, with fatal consequences.

If you are keeping the birds on a colony system, allow for several more nestboxes than you have breeding pairs of cockatiels. This should help to prevent nest-sharing, which invariably leads to losses of eggs and chicks. Position all the boxes at a similar height, otherwise the birds are likely to favour the higher ones.

It is important to fix all nestboxes securely in place using brackets. Support the main weight of the box on an L-shaped bracket fitted onto the base of the box and the adjoining part of the flight framework. Make sure that the screws on the outside of the nestbox do not penetrate within, otherwise they could damage the eggs inside.

Site the nestbox in a sheltered spot under cover in the outside flight. Be sure that no rain can penetrate the roof, since a heavy downpour could saturate the interior and cause the adult birds to desert their nest. At the same time, the nestbox must be reasonably accessible, so that you can inspect it with minimum disturbance.

Above: *A cock balances on the hen's back when mating. One mating will fertilize a full clutch.*

Nest lining

The nest lining is an important consideration. Although damp peat is favoured by some breeders, it is not entirely satisfactory. The cockatiels often scrape the peat out of the nestbox, and if the hen lays on the bare floor, the eggs are likely to roll about, becoming chilled or damaged as a result.

It is much better for the cockatiels to prepare their own nest lining. Provide thin softwood battening for this purpose, cut into pieces about 5cm(2in) long. The cockatiels will gnaw this down to produce a suitable floor covering for the nestbox. Watch their progress, however, and provide more wood as it is gnawed away. Only a thin layer is required as a lining, otherwise there is a risk that the eggs may be buried.

Breeding behaviour

Breeding starts with both the male and female cockatiel investigating the inside of the nestbox. Then you will notice the cock bird displaying outside the box; he will sing to attract the attention of the hen inside, holding his wings slightly away from his body. Once she is ready to mate, she will in turn respond by flattening herself against the perch, allowing the cock to mount her. Mating is most likely to occur when the hen leaves the nestbox and the cock is in the flight nearby. Although only one successful mating is needed to fertilize the clutch of eggs, cockatiels have been observed to mate repeatedly.

Just before egg laying, the hen will spend much longer in the nestbox, having vigorously whittled away the cuttlefish bone. Her droppings often become larger at this stage. The first egg is usually laid ten to fourteen days after the nestbox is hung in place, but hens have been known to lay much more rapidly. Obviously, much depends on the condition of each hen bird. If the nestbox is withheld for too long, it is not unusual for hens to lay either in a food pot or, more commonly, from a perch, so that the egg smashes on the floor.

During the laying period the hen remains largely on her own in the nestbox. The usual clutch consists of about five eggs, laid on alternate days, although the number can range from two up to seven. In colony aviaries, ten or more of the white eggs may be found in the nestbox. This is likely to be the result of cohabiting by two hens, however, rather than the output of a single individual. Because cockatiels cannot incubate this number of eggs successfully, some are certain to be chilled and will fail to hatch as a result.

Incubation does not usually start until after the hen has produced at least two eggs. When the clutch is complete, both cock and hen take turns at sitting on the eggs. Generally speaking, the cock incubates during the day, while the hen sits overnight. Young cocks sometimes refuse to accept their share of this duty and the clutch may be abandoned, but normally the problem resolves itself in time. There is nothing that can be done to entice the cock to incubate; the only option is to foster the eggs to another pair, preferably laying at the same time. This ensures there will be no great discrepancy in the size of the chicks when they hatch.

The average incubation period for the cockatiel is nineteen days, but it can be longer, depending partly on when incubation began. The parent birds sometimes eject eggshells from the nestbox, which should confirm the presence of one or more chicks inside. Newly hatched cockatiels are covered in a dense layer of fluffy, normally yellowish down. The albino is an exception, however, having white down and, as with other red-eyed varieties, its distinctive eye coloration is evident even at this stage, before the eyes open.

Young cockatiels are vociferous, especially when being fed, and this provides a means of keeping a check on their progress. Established pairs do not resent regular nest inspection and some breeders routinely inspect nestboxes every day. Others prefer to leave the cockatiels without any interference, unless they suspect that something is wrong.

Whichever approach you follow, never open a nestbox containing chicks while one or both adults are also inside. This causes a mad scramble that will inevitably injure the chicks. You can often persuade adult cockatiels to leave the nestbox simply by offering them greenfood. This gives you an opportunity to look at the chicks without disturbing the adult birds. Alternatively, if the parent is still sitting tight, tap gently on the side of the nestbox, and this should encourage the cockatiel to emerge without harming the chicks at all.

By the time they are one week old, young cockatiels should be rocking back and forth, hissing rather like their parents if disturbed in the nestbox. Their eyes will just be starting to open, and their feathers will be emerging from the skin. Mortality can be quite high in young nestling cockatiels; the youngest member of a clutch is the most vulnerable, especially once the adult birds cease brooding the chicks. Given access to a nestbox, cockatiels will continue to lay for much of the year but, not surprisingly, breeding results during the colder months can be very poor, because the chicks can easily become chilled.

Hand rearing cockatiels
Regular inspection of the nestbox can provide an early indication of problems, enabling you to take appropriate action. If, for example, the youngest chick appears to be falling behind its nestmates, you can provide it with supplementary food. Two daily feeds, given in the morning and evening, can ensure the survival of a neglected chick. Reduce the time that the chick is away from the nestbox by preparing the food before you remove the chick. Offer the food on a teaspoon with the edges bent inwards to form a funnel, rather than in a syringe. A spoon allows the chick to feed at its own pace, whereas pressure on the syringe

can force too much food into the chick's mouth, causing it to choke.

After feeding, always wipe the chick's beak carefully to remove any deposits of food. If allowed to adhere to the soft tissue of the beak the food could cause permanent distortion in later life.

The crop at the base of the neck gives a clear indication of whether or not a chick has recently been fed. Hungry youngsters have slack crops, whereas a full crop appears whitish in colour compared with the surrounding skin. When you are feeding a chick continue until the crop appears quite full, but not at bursting point! Young cockatiels will probably need feeding every three hours or so, with a slightly longer gap overnight. Never allow their crops to empty completely, but top them up at regular intervals.

Top: *A clutch of cockatiel eggs.* Centre: *A group of newly hatched lutino chicks. Their eyes are still closed, but the coloration is clearly red.* Left: *The crest feathers are just becoming evident by the time they are 10 days old.* Below: *The body plumage is well developed at about 16 days. At this stage, young birds are vulnerable to feather plucking by the adults (see also page 50).*

Unlike most parrots, young cockatiels do not actively gape for food, but move their heads in a bobbing fashion to elicit food from the adult bird. This can make feeding slightly more difficult, until you are used to it.

It is obviously much easier if the adult cockatiels continue to look after their youngsters, even if some supplementary feeding is required. Sometimes, however, you will need to take over the entire task of rearing a chick and then you will need to keep the young cockatiels warm in a brooder. Newly hatched chicks need to be kept at about 37°C(99°F), gradually reduced to

Above: *In an unfeathered chick the crop is obvious just below the throat. This youngster is being well fed. The eyes are starting to open.*

around 27°C(80°F), by the time the youngest is nearly two weeks old. Monitor the temperature using an internal thermometer.

A clean, empty plastic container, such as a margarine tub makes a suitable receptacle for young cockatiels at first, but more spacious containers will be required as they grow bigger. Line the receptacle with paper towelling and be sure to change this bedding regularly after each feed.

Below: *Applying a closed ring. The first step is to bunch the three longest toes carefully together.*

Below: *With the toes held in place, slide a closed ring of the right diameter to the centre of the foot.*

Ringing

Birdkeepers are divided in their attitudes towards ringing chicks. The disruption involved can result in nervous parents neglecting their offspring, but it does provide a vital means of identifying individual birds at a later date. This can be especially important in breeding programmes, where accurate information and record keeping concerning the parentage and age of the cockatiels is vital.

If you do decide to close-ring the chicks with circular bands, usually made of aluminium, do this when each bird is nine or ten days old. If left any longer, the toes of the young birds will have grown too large, making it impossible to slide the band over them. The internal dimension for cockatiel rings is 5mm(0.2in), thus ensuring that they should fit comfortably around the leg when the bird is adult. Unfortunately, some rings do occasionally cause the leg to swell up and must be removed without delay, otherwise the circulation to the toes will be affected and gangrene will set in. Seek the assistance of a veterinarian, who will have special tools to cut the ring off the leg. Once the pressure is removed, the swelling should subside and the cockatiel will not suffer any lasting ill-effects.

If you do operate a banding scheme, it is important to keep good records in the form of a breeding register. This will enable you to trace the ancestry of a particular cockatiel by its ring number. Alternatively, you can use split plastic rings simply for identification purposes. These can be numbered in the same way as closed bands and, since they can be applied to the bird's leg at any stage, there is no need to disturb the chicks during the breeding period in order to put them on.

Remove the chicks from the aviary to another flight or a cage as soon as they are eating on their own. They normally emerge from the nestbox at between four and five weeks old, and should be independent about a fortnight later. This is a good time to apply split rings, as the chicks will have to be caught up in any case at this stage. Be sure to close split rings carefully after applying them, so the cockatiels do not become caught up in their quarters in the future.

Allow the adult cockatiels to rear two rounds of chicks in succession, and then remove the nestboxes; otherwise they will continue breeding, usually with less satisfactory results. After the breeding season, it it a good idea to deworm adult birds as a matter of routine (see page 47). Clean out the aviary very thoroughly to eliminate red mites, and make any necessary repairs to the structure before the onset of winter. Then, early in the following year, repeat the deworming and cleaning procedures before replacing the nestboxes. In this way, the next season's chicks will be less exposed to infection when they emerge from the nest.

Below: *Pass the ring over the little toe. Be sure to carry out ringing before the foot is too large.*

Below: *Use a blunt matchstick to free the little toe. Finally, check that the ring slides easily.*

Cockatiel genetics

In order to breed a specific cockatiel variety successfully, it is important to know something about the bird's genetic make-up. In practical terms, this also means understanding how the colour concerned is transmitted from one generation to the next. Here, we look briefly at the basic mechanisms involved and then consider a number of case studies that show genetics – literally the 'science of inheritance' – in action.

How genes are transmitted
Within the nucleus of each living cell, the genes, or 'inherited characters', are present on structures called chromosomes. Each chromosome has an identical 'partner', so that the total number is made up of two sets of 'partners'. (Only the female sex chromosomes fail to fit into this neat arrangement – see below.) During the reproductive phase, when the sperm and egg meet, one set of chromosomes (i.e. half of the normal number) from each of the parents come together to form new pairs in the resulting offspring. This ensures that the offspring receive chromosomes, and therefore genes, from both parents.

Because some genes are dominant, however, they can mask so-called recessive genes present on the adjoining chromosome. In the case of coloration, only these dominant genes will have a visible effect on the bird's appearance. As a result, it is possible for the appearance of the cockatiel (its phenotype) to differ from its genetic make-up (its genotype).

When the corresponding genes differ, the cockatiel is said to be heterozygous, or 'split', for the character concerned. Two corresponding genes that are the same – irrespective of whether they are both dominant or recessive – are said to be homozygous.

Within the nucleus, a special pair of chromosomes – the so-called sex chromosomes – determines the bird's gender. (The remaining 'non-sex' chromosomes are called autosomes.) Studying these under

Above: *Understanding cockatiel genetics is important if you are interested in breeding colour varieties, such as this white-faced silver, one of the new forms (see pages 86-92).*

a microscope forms the basis of sexing birds by chromosomal karyotyping. The sex chromosomes of a hen are described as ZY, with the Y referring to the shorter member of the pair. Those of the cock are known as ZZ and are of equal length. This distinction is particularly significant when breeding for mutations that occur on the sex chromosomes.

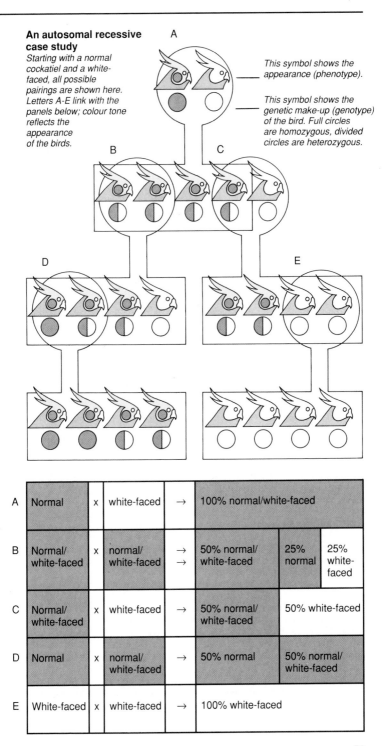

An autosomal recessive case study

Starting with a normal cockatiel and a white-faced, all possible pairings are shown here. Letters A-E link with the panels below; colour tone reflects the appearance of the birds.

This symbol shows the appearance (phenotype).

This symbol shows the genetic make-up (genotype) of the bird. Full circles are homozygous, divided circles are heterozygous.

A	Normal	x	white-faced	→	100% normal/white-faced		
B	Normal/white-faced	x	normal/white-faced	→	50% normal/white-faced	25% normal	25% white-faced
C	Normal/white-faced	x	white-faced	→	50% normal/white-faced	50% white-faced	
D	Normal	x	normal/white-faced	→	50% normal	50% normal/white-faced	
E	White-faced	x	white-faced	→	100% white-faced		

An autosomal recessive case study

This group of mutations occurs on the autosomes, and are recessive to the normal form of the cockatiel. In this case, when you mate a recessive mutant to a normal cockatiel, all the offspring resemble the normal in appearance, but they will carry the recessive mutation in their genotype. It is impossible to distinguish between the normal (homozygous) and split (heterozygous) offspring without suitable trial pairings.

The white-faced mutant is one of the most recent colour forms that fits into this category. The panel shows all the possible pairings for this mutation with the normal form. Only the first and third pairings will produce normals that can be guaranteed to be split for white-faced. In all other cases, the offspring could be either normal or split. If mating an apparently normal cockatiel with a white-faced produces any white-faced offspring, this proves that the normal is split for the white-faced characteristic. Similarly, if two apparently normal cockatiels produce white-faced offspring (or indeed any of the autosomal recessive mutations), then they must both be split for the character concerned.

The other known mutations with the same mode of inheritance are the pied, the recessive silver and the fallow cockatiel.

A sex-linked recessive case study

Here, the recessive mutation affects genes located only on the pair of sex chromosomes. In this case, hens, which have one shorter chromosome, can only carry one of the genes. Therefore, their phenotype must match their genotype. Cocks, on the other hand, have two sex chromosomes of equal length and thus can still be split for the character concerned.

If you can only acquire one mutant member for a pair of this type of mutation, concentrate on keeping mutant cocks. You will then be certain of breeding a

A sex-linked recessive case study

Pearl cock	x	normal hen
Normal cock	x	pearl hen
Pearl cock	x	pearl hen
Normal/ pearl cock	x	normal hen
Normal/ pearl cock	x	pearl hen

A dominant case study

Dominant silver (df)	x	normal
Dominant silver (sf)	x	normal
Dominant silver (df)	x	dominant silver (df)
Dominant silver (sf)	x	dominant silver (sf)
Dominant silver (df)	x	dominant silver (sf)

proportion of mutant hens. This important distinction can be seen by contrasting the first and second pairings in the panel illustrating the pearl mutation. In this specific case, you may be able to recognize normal cockatiels that are split for pearl, by examining the plumage under the wing, near the shoulder. Slight streaking here indicates a heterozygous cockatiel. This method does not work with the lutino and cinnamon, the other two

→	50% normal/pearl cocks		50% pearl hens	
→	50% normal/pearl cocks		50% normal hens	
→	50% pearl cocks		50% pearl hens	
→	25% normal cocks	25% normal/pearl cocks	25% normal hens	25% pearl hens
→	25% normal/pearl cocks	25% pearl cocks	25% normal hens	25% pearl hens

→	100% dominant silver (sf)	
→	50% dominant silver (sf)	50% normal
→	100% dominant silver (df)	
→	50% dominant silver (sf)	25% dominant silver (df)	25% normal
→	50% dominant silver (df)	50% dominant silver (sf)

sex-linked mutations; it is impossible to distinguish the splits visually in these colours.

A dominant case study

There is only one mutation known to be dominant in cockatiels – the dominant silver. The essential difference in this case is that dominant-coloured offspring should result in the first generation, although the relative proportions will depend on whether the cockatiel is a single factor (sf) or double factor (df) individual. This is a direct reflection of whether one or both chromosomes carry mutant genes. It should be possible to distinguish these birds visually, since double factor individuals are lighter in colour than their single factor counterparts. As the panel shows, if normal offspring appear from mating a dominant silver with a normal then the mutant cockatiel must be a single factor individual.

Colour varieties

The cockatiel differs in its coloration from most members of the parrot family because of the absence of the so-called 'blue layer' in its plumage. In cockatiels, two groups of colour pigment are present; yellow coloration and orange markings on the cheek patches occur because of pigment present in the outer layer of the feather, and darker markings result from melanin pigments at a deeper level in the feather.

In most parrots, there is an intervening blue layer, with the result that when melanin is absent, the blue and yellow properties of the feather combine to create the impression of green. Since this is not feasible in cockatiels, the mutation that removes melanin results in a yellowish bird with red eyes – the lutino. Conversely, when the yellow and orange coloration are removed from the plumage, these areas turn white, creating the white-faced cockatiel. In this case, there are no cheek patches present, of course, but adult hens retain the characteristic barring on the tail. However, instead of the usual yellow coloration, the barring appears as white.

A partial loss of either set of pigments gives rise to pied cockatiels, with areas of pale yellow or white plumage irregularly scattered over the whole body, including the wings and tail. In the pearl mutation, there is a very localized inability to produce melanin in the centre of the individual feathers. This creates a scalloped appearance, so that pearl cockatiels have feathers with light centres and darker lacing around their edges. The situation usually alters in adult cock birds, however, because as they mature they produce more melanin, which compensates for the shortfall arising as a result of the mutation (see also page 79).

Melanin pigments are also affected in cinnamon and silver mutations. In cinnamon cockatiels it becomes modified, turning brownish, while the yellow and orange markings are essentially unaffected. A dilution of melanin underlies the appearance of the silver forms of the cockatiel.

A combination of these various changes is apparent in the different colour forms. The pearl lutino, for example, has no melanin, and is

Pigmentation in the feather

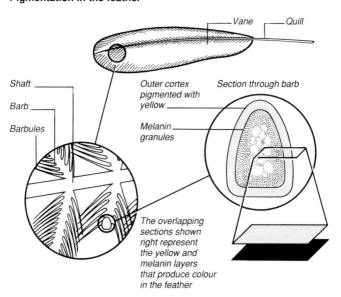

Vane — Quill

Shaft

Barb

Barbules

Outer cortex pigmented with yellow

Melanin granules

Section through barb

The overlapping sections shown right represent the yellow and melanin layers that produce colour in the feather

How the colours are built up

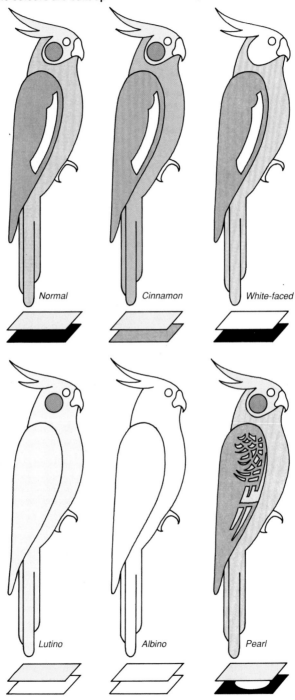

Normal

Cinnamon

White-faced

Lutino

Albino

Pearl

thus an attractive shade of yellow, with white edging betraying pearl markings. Since there is no pigment present in the albino, it is impossible to create any combinations around this variety.

Future trends

The growing interest in cockatiels stems partly from the development of the various colours. Whereas several colours of budgerigar are known to have been seen first in flocks in Australia, no mutation of the cockatiel has ever been recorded from the wild.

In their native habitat, cockatiels range widely over frequently inhospitable terrain in search of food and water. They have evolved their powerful flight to enable them to cover these large distances; at the same time, their rapid and high reproductive capacity is an essential ingredient for the survival of the species in a region where rainfall – and therefore a supply of grasses and other greenfood – can be highly unpredictable.

At present, the natural appearance of the cockatiel has been little altered by selective breeding, in noticeable contrast to the budgerigar. However, this could change quite rapidly as increasing numbers of cockatiels are exhibited. Should the trend favour larger cockatiels on the show bench, then breeders will obviously aim to conform to such requirements. This carries with it a risk that the natural grace and elegance of the cockatiel will be lost in a stampede for size in exhibition birds. Thankfully, this does not appear to be the case at present, but the risk remains, especially while there are no official standards for exhibition cockatiels laid down in many countries.

Showing

If you are interested in showing your cockatiels, try to visit some local shows and speak to breeders first. All exhibition birds, irrespective of their coloration, must be in top condition, with a full complement of claws. Do not

Above: *The dominant silver is the only cockatiel mutation known to be dominant in its mode of inheritance. A similar type of pied mutation may arise in the future, as in budgies.*

Right: *Depth of yellow and extent of darker markings varies in pieds.*

exhibit moulting cockatiels, as they will not be in perfect feather condition, an essential prerequisite for success. Depending on where you live in the world, it may be necessary to exhibit cockatiels in special show cages.

Ensure that the birds selected for the show are all steady and accustomed to their quarters, so that they will not be nervous when being judged. Training young cockatiels for exhibition purposes is strongly recommended, and you can start the process almost as soon as they are separated from their parents. Tame birds are also likely to make better breeding stock, so the effort you put into training them is never wasted.

The colours

On the following pages we examine in more detail all the primary colour mutations and the colour combinations bred from them. For easy reference they are listed in alphabetical order of primary colour. Although no clear-cut nomenclature exists at present for the various cockatiel colour combinations, it seems sensible to adopt a system similar to that used for budgerigars. Therefore, we have chosen to describe the colour marking first, followed by the colour so that, for example, 'pearl lutino' is preferred to 'lutino pearl'.

Right: **Normal grey**
An adult pair. The cock on the left can be easily distinguished by its bright yellow facial markings.

Below: **Normal grey cock**
In some birds, the normal grey coloration of the plumage is more intense than in others.

Cinnamon

This mutation was established in Belgium by the late 1960s, and breeders in Europe, but not in the UK, still sometimes refer to it as the Isabelle. Cinnamons can vary quite widely in depth of coloration, with adult cocks being darker because of the natural presence of more melanin in their plumage.

A warm, even shade of cinnamon is usually preferred. Both the legs and eyes are lighter in coloration than those of normal cockatiels. Sexing birds is simple after the first moult, with cocks acquiring dark rather than barred undersides to their tail feathers.

Right: **Cinnamon hen**
These birds have a warm, brownish tinge to their plumage. Adult hens retain their barred tail feathers.

Below: **Cinnamon cock**
Some cinnamon cockatiels are much paler than others. This is a sex-linked mutation (see page 60).

Far right: **Primrose pearl (lacewing) cinnamon**
Attractive coloration combines with delicate markings in this hen bird.

Right: **Dilute cinnamon pied hen**
Here, the cinnamon coloration is reduced in intensity, producing an elegant 'creamy' coloured bird.

Below: **Pearl (lacewing) cinnamon**
Sexing may be more difficult in pearl forms because of the partial absence of melanin. This is a hen.

Dominant silver

The most recent cockatiel mutation, the dominant silver, is also the only one to date to have emerged in the UK. It was discovered by chance in a pet shop during 1979, by a keen breeder. He was able to trace the original pair that had produced this unusual cockatiel, only to discover that the cock had died. But pairing the young cock back to its mother yielded three further silver offspring in 1980. All proved to be cocks. Then, by a careful process of inbreeding (pairing closely related birds together) and outcrossing (introducing unrelated cockatiels to the breeding stock), the mutation was successfully developed.

Dominant silver cockatiels are likely to become increasingly common in the near future. Their silver coloration is darkish around the base of the neck, extending up onto the head, whereas their yellow and orange markings are unaffected. They cannot be separated from normals in the nest until they start to feather up. Silvers then appear paler, with a brownish tinge to their plumage, while their eyes and legs are black. Adult coloration is assumed at the first moult, although some hens may remain slightly darker than cocks. Selective breeding may lead to the establishment of paler strains.

Single and double factor dominant silver cockatiels can be separated by their coloration. Double factor birds are significantly lighter than single factor birds, being similar to a lutino, but with a grey overlay. They retain the darker head markings, and the black coloration of the eyes and feet.

Mating dominant silvers with

Right: **Dominant silver cock**
This single factor form is more common and darker in coloration. Facial markings are retained.

Below: **Dominant silver cock**
This is a double factor bird. It is lighter in coloration than the single factor dominant silver. An increasingly popular mutation.

other mutations will, in the first instance, produce splits that can then be used to develop other colour varieties. One of the most striking created to date has been the white-faced dominant silver, in which all trace of yellow and orange plumage is absent. This has been named platinum, in view of its metallic coloration.

Above: **Dominant silver hen**
This single factor hen bird is recognizable by its greyish face.

Right: **White-faced silver cock**
A recent mutation. It has also become known as the platinum.

Fallow

Since its first appearance in 1971, in the collection of a Florida breeder, this mutation has tended to remain better known in the United States than in Europe. Fallow cockatiels have red eyes and a greyish yellow body coloration that distinguishes them from cinnamons. The mode of inheritance is also different, because this is an autosomal recessive, rather than a sex-linked recessive mutation. (See *Cockatiel genetics* starting on page 58 for a full explanation of the mechanisms involved.) Once again, however, the depth of coloration does vary: cocks are generally darker.

Below: **Fallow hen**
This is one of the more subtle of the current mutations and it remains a rare form at the present time.

Lutino

Undoubtedly, the most popular cockatiel mutation – the lutino – also originated in the United States. It arose in the aviaries of a Florida breeder in 1958 and the strain was then developed successfully by another breeder, Mrs Moon. Although these early 'moonbeams' sold for vast sums of money, lutinos are now available at low cost, having been bred in vast numbers around the world.

Until the emergence of the genuine albino (see page 86), breeders often used to describe lutinos incorrectly under this name, or sometimes as whites. Because

they lack just the melanin pigment, however, these birds are, by definition, lutinos. Part of the reason for the confusion stemmed from the pale coloration, bordering on white, of many lutinos. Those that show the darkest shade of yellow are usually preferred.

It is possible to influence the depth of coloration to some extent by choosing the best-coloured individuals and pairing these together. In order to indicate the depth of coloration, breeders sometimes use 'primrose' and 'buttercup' as prefixes, and describe the darker coloured cockatiels as buttercup lutinos. A truly rich yellow colour is, however, rarely achieved in practice.

A genetic flaw closely associated with the lutino mutation is the presence of a bald patch on the head, immediately behind the crest. Do not pair such cockatiels together, otherwise this characteristic will soon become widespread throughout your stud.

It is also possible to create attractive pearl lutinos, which were first bred during the mid-1970s. If you buy a single pearl lutino, make sure that you obtain a cock bird. Then, when you pair this bird with a lutino hen, you will breed pearl lutino hens and lutino cocks split for pearl. No visual pearl lutinos will result from the reverse pairing.

It is not worth attempting to create pied lutinos, because the lutino character has already removed the melanin essential for producing pied markings.

Left: **Lutino**
Carefully studying the underside of the tails of lutinos is the only way to sex adult birds accurately. Barring is still present in hens. Although rare at first, this popular form is widely available today.

Right: **Pearl lutinos**
In lutino birds, no melanin pigment is present, hence the attractive yellow coloration. The pearl mutation provides the deeper yellow markings which, in these birds, is most apparent on the wings.

Pearl

The pearl cockatiel was first bred in 1967 in West Germany. The scalloped patterning can be very variable; it may be confined largely to the back and wings, or it can extend onto the breast as well. Where melanin is absent from the centre of the individual feathers, this area can vary in colour from white through to yellow, and the cockatiels are then described either as silver or golden pearls. There is no consistency in this regard; chicks of both types may appear in the same nest. The situation is further complicated by the use of the term 'lacewing' to describe pearl cockatiels with a more elongated pattern of markings.

Until recently, it was accepted that cock pearl cockatiels lost their distinctive markings when they moulted into adult plumage, by about nine months old. However, it now appears that in the United States selective breeding has led to the development of a strain in which adult cock birds do not produce more melanin. They therefore retain their pearl markings even when they are mature. As well as pearl lutinos, the pearl form of the cinnamon is an attractive colour variant and can be bred in a similar fashion. See page 76 for more information on breeding pearl cockatiels.

Above: **Primrose pearl (lacewing) hen**
The term 'lacewing' is used for pearl cockatiels in which the markings are elongated rather than circular. A strikingly marked bird.

Left: **Pearl hen**
The pearl markings result from a shortage of melanin in the centre of individual feathers. Hens retain their appearance, but adult pearl cocks often moult out like normals.

Right: **Pearl silver cock**
In this cock bird, pearl markings and the silver mutation combine to produce this unusually coloured bird. This cockatiel is moulting, hence the short tail feathers.

Pied

Pieds, the oldest of the cockatiel mutations, were being bred in California as long ago as 1949. Unfortunately, it is impossible to predict the extent of the pied markings. While some birds are very similar to normals, others may be recognized by the presence of just a few grey feathers in otherwise pale yellow plumage. The trend among birdkeepers appears to favour pieds in which one quarter of the plumage is dark grey and the remainder is clear. Symmetry of the markings is also preferred, but hard to achieve.

It can also be difficult to sex pieds, because the pied markings may obscure the usual plumage differences. Nevertheless, cock birds can usually be recognized by their characteristic song. Various colour combinations have now been developed, with cinnamon pieds being among the most attractive. If you pair a pied cinnamon cock to a normal pied hen, half the resulting offspring should be pied cinnamon hens, which can be sexed at this stage. The other chicks will be normal pied cocks, all split for cinnamon.

Pearl pieds have also been bred, as have pearl pied cinnamons, which combine all three mutations on a single cockatiel. The latter variety was first produced in Texas in 1980, but it has proved difficult to balance the markings as required for show purposes. Pairing a pearl cock split for cinnamon to a pearl pied hen should result in a proportion of the offspring being of this particular variety.

Right: **Pearl pied cock**
Here, the pied markings are most evident on the head and neck. The extent of the piedness varies, even between individual nestmates.

Below: **Pearl pieds**
A pair, with the adult cock on the right showing the typical loss of pearling. This results from the greater production of melanin that occurs after the bird matures.

Above: **Primrose pied cock**
The term 'primrose' is used to describe cockatiels with a light shade of yellow coloration.

Top right: **Primrose pearl cinnamon pieds**
An attractive pair, but their chicks may be more heavily marked.

Bottom right: **Primrose pearl cinnamon pied**
Three separate mutations have been combined to produce this striking variety. The depth of the primrose coloration may be improved by mating together darker yellow birds. Unusual colour forms are advertised in hobbyist magazines.

Left: **Cinnamon pied**
*This cock bird has a limited amount
of light variegation. Cinnamon
pieds are a popular mutation.*

Below: **White-faced pied**
*The pied markings on this cock bird
show as white areas, and in this
bird the beak is also affected.*

Recessive silver

Silver cockatiels have a long history. They were first recorded in New Zealand at the start of the 1950s, but that strain was never established and today's recessive silvers are of European origin. Here they were bred in the latter years of the 1960s, but the original examples were often afflicted with blindness from an early age. Their eye coloration is red, which distinguishes them visually from the dominant silver cockatiel.

Although the problem of blindness has been overcome, this recessive mutation remains scarce. Its future development is likely to suffer further as a result of the establishment of the dominant silver, because breeding those cockatiels is genetically easier.

White-faced

The development of this mutation is equivalent to the breeding of a blue budgerigar, and has paved the way for the subsequent development of the albino cockatiel. The white-faced was first recorded in Holland in about 1969. By the late 1970s it had been bred in Germany, and reached the UK at about this time.

Although the yellow coloration and orange cheek patches are absent in this mutation, it is still possible to sex adults easily. Most hens have barred tails and greyish, rather than white faces. A possible exception may exist among white-faced pieds, where this coloration can be disrupted.

Various other combinations have been developed, including cinnamon and pearl forms. The most significant is the albino, which was probably first bred in Germany

Right: **White-faced cock**
Yellow coloration and orange markings are absent from the plumage in this attractive mutation, but the male is easily recognizable by its white face.

Below: **White-faced hen**
This autosomal recessive mutation is becoming increasingly common. Hen birds have greyish faces and retain the barred tail markings.

in about 1980. This variety is the result of combining white-faced and lutino cockatiels in two stages. First, mate a lutino cock to a white-faced hen, to yield lutino/white-faced hens. It is also necessary to pair a white-faced/lutino cock to a lutino hen, producing lutino/white-faced cocks. Pairing these offspring together should produce a one-in-four chance of breeding an albino in this second generation.

Because the combination of chromosomes occurs entirely by chance, you may find more than one albino in a nest or, on the other hand, you may find none! However, the likelihood of an albino chick is increased as more chicks are produced, so over a breeding season you would be unlucky not to breed at least one albino bird.

Right: **Albino**
This is one of the most recent and highly prized colour varieties, bred using white-faced and lutino stock. These birds are pure white, as they lack all colour pigment. Their popularity seems assured.

Below: **White-faced cinnamon pied hen**
Here, the presence of scattered white feathers over the bird's wings, outside the normal white area, confirms that it is a pied. The tail barring is also white.

Above: **Pearl (lacewing) white-faced cinnamon**
Because the yellow group of pigments is missing in all colour combinations involving the white-faced mutation, loss of melanin produces white rather than pale yellow facial markings. In hens, as here, the face is greyish.

Right: **Pearl white-faced pied**
The pied markings on this cock bird are clearly visible on the head, with pearl markings on the wings.

Overleaf: **Pearl white-faced hen**
A striking white-faced mutation. Symmetry of markings may be desirable, but is hard to achieve.

Other colours

Cockatiels showing other markings and coloration have been recorded from time to time, but none appear established. It may be that some plumage changes are the result of metabolic disturbances and are not of genetic origin, so they cannot be described as true mutations. This probably explains the occasional cockatiel with orange rather than yellow crest feathers, although there is rumoured to be a totally orange bird in Europe!

A few cockatiels with an olive greenish tinge to their plumage have also been documented. They derive from cinnamon strains of birds and it seems that an excessive degree of yellowing, in combination with cinnamon, may create this unusual appearance.

A more conventional mutation may prove to be the clear-flight, with white flight feathers, a mutation that already exists in the budgerigar. Looking to the future, a mutation may arise that darkens the melanin, so that a black cockatiel could be developed. Whatever happens in this field, however, the popularity of the cockatiel is likely to continue growing for the foreseeable future.

Below: **Café au lait**
Not a new mutation, but a pale form of the cinnamon, developed in Europe. Breeders continue to research into new colour varieties.

Index

Page numbers in **bold** indicate major references including accompanying photographs. Page numbers in *italics* indicate captions to other illustrations. Less important text entries are shown in normal type.